IN THE FOOTSTEPS
THE QUIET MAI

Turned down by all the major film companies, **THE QUIET MAN** brought together John Wayne and Maureen O'Hara for only the second time on screen, won two Oscars and was showered with both critical and popular praise on both sides of the Atlantic. Even today, its world-wide video sales are quite outstanding.

THE QUIET MAN is rightly hailed as a Holywood classic. Set in the 1920s and shot in the 1950s, the timeless, fairy-tale character of director John Ford's Ireland is as captivating now as it ever was.

GERRY McNEE first saw the movie when he was very young and it has intrigued him ever since. *In the Footsteps of* **THE QUIET MAN** is a tribute to the film and all those involved in its making, for the story behind the story, the off-screen drama, is a fascinating tale in itself. McNee has researched his subject thoroughly and conducted countless interviews to produce a stimulating and compulsive homage to what critic and author Andrew Sarris called 'a retreat into the pastoral and horse-drawn past [but] very much ahead of its time . . .'. It is a revealing and touching account of when Hollywood came to beautiful Connemara in the West of Ireland.

Fascinating, funny, revelatory . . . for once an upbeat slice of film history.
Shaun Usher, *Daily Mail*

Fans of the film world will delight in this anecdotal account.
Glasgow Herald

Innisfree Guided Tours now make daily visits to all the locations in and around Cong used in John Ford's classic movie *The Quiet Man*.

The tour includes the entrance fee into the beautiful grounds of the world famous Ashford Castle Hotel, and gives an in-depth account of the story and all the locations used in the filming of this masterpiece.

See the houses of Red Will Danaher and the Reverend Playfair, and where Dan Tobin was raised from the dead. Stop at Pat Cohan's bar and Curran's pub, wander around Innisfree and see where such famous events as the Fight Scene took place, and where Sean Thornton and Mary Kate Danaher (otherwise known as John Wayne and Maureen O'Hara) rode their tandem and went a-courting. You also get a certificate at the end of the tour, with a chance to join The Quiet Man Locations Fan Club.

It is a must for all *Quiet Man* enthusiasts and tickets are available from: The Quiet Man Locations Ticket Office, Abbey Street, Cong, Co. Mayo, Ireland. Tel: (092) 46089.

IN THE FOOTSTEPS OF
THE QUIET MAN

GERRY McNEE

MAINSTREAM
PUBLISHING

To
Mum and Dad

Copyright © Gerry McNee, 1990
All rights reserved
First published in Great Britain 1990 by
MAINSTREAM PUBLISHING COMPANY (EDINBURGH)
LTD
7 Albany Street
Edinburgh EH1 3UG

ISBN 1 85158 321 1
Reprinted 1991

Pictures courtesy of the Connacht Tribune and Irish Times Ltd. Front cover picture courtesy of Irish Film Institute

British Library Cataloguing in Publication Data

McNee, Gerry
In the footsteps of 'The Quiet Man'.
1. British cinema films. Making
I. Title
791.430232
ISBN 1–85158–321–1

Typeset in 11 on 13 pt Bembo by Selectmove
Printed and bound in Great Britain by
Billings and Sons Ltd, Worcester

CONTENTS

Acknowledgments

My thanks to Mr Charles FitzSimons, Executive Director of the Producers' Guild of America, for carefully reading the manuscript and suggesting improvements. His interest in this book was most welcome as he appeared in *The Quiet Man*, was involved in much of its planning and is none other than brother of Maureen O'Hara. My thanks also to Lord and Lady Killanin not just for opening their considerable files to me but also their home. Their courtesy, patience and hospitality were greatly appreciated. Also Pat Woods, arguably the best librarian in the business, for much personal help. James Bradshaw for his coveted copy of *Green Rushes*. The staffs of the National Library in Dublin, the Mitchell Library in Glasgow, the Lilly Library, Indiana University, USA, Sunniva O'Flynn at the Irish Film Institute in Dublin, Carmel Sheehy at *The Connacht Tribune* in Galway, the RTE video library staff in Dublin, The Irish Tourist Board, The Abbey Theatre Press Office in Dublin, *The Irish Times, The Sunday World*, the staff of Ashford Castle, Mildred Natwick, J. J. Murphy, J. A. Fahy, Robert Foy, my guide in and around Cong, and the wonderful people of that village for their warmth, friendship and tremendous help.

A REPUBLIC PRODUCTION

Herbert J. Yates presents – John Ford and Merian C. Cooper's
Argosy Production, *THE QUIET MAN*

STARRING
John Wayne, Maureen O'Hara, Barry Fitzgerald . . . with Ward
Bond, Victor McLaglen, Mildred Natwick, Francis Ford

IRISH PLAYERS
Eileen Crowe, May Craig, Arthur Shields, Charles FitzSimons,
James Lilburn, Sean McClory, Jack McGowran, Joseph O'Dea,
Eric Gorman, Kevin Lawless, Paddy O'Donnell
Screenplay by Frank S. Nugent
From the story by Maurice Walsh
Music, Victor Young
Colour by Technicolor
Director of Photography, Winton C. Hoch ASC
Technicolor Colour Consultant, Francis Cugat
2nd Unit Photography, Archie Stout ASC
Art Director, Frank Hotaling
Film Editor, Jack Murray ACE
Sound, T. A. Carman, Howard Wilson
Costumes, Adele Palmer
Set decorations, John McCarthy Jr., Charles Thompson
RCA Sound System
Directed by John Ford

A fuller cast list tracked down shows the following:

JOHN WAYNE   *Sean Thornton*
MAUREEN O'HARA   *Mary Kate Danaher*
BARRY FITZGERALD   *Michaeleen Oge Flynn*
WARD BOND   *Father Peter Lonergan*
VICTOR McLAGLEN   *Red Will Danaher*
MILDRED NATWICK   *Mrs Sarah Tillane*
FRANCIS FORD   *Dan Tobin*
EILEEN CROWE   *Mrs Elizabeth Playfair*
MAY CRAIG   *Woman at railroad station*
ARTHUR SHIELDS   *Reverend Cyril Playfair*

CHARLES FITZSIMONS *Forbes*
SEAN McCLORY *Owen Glynn*
JAMES LILBURN *Father Paul*
JACK McGOWRAN *Feeney*
KEN CURTIS *Dermot Fahy*
MAE MARSH *Father Paul's mother*
HARRY TENBROOK *Policeman*
MAJOR SAM HARRIS *General*
JOSEPH O'DEA *Train driver*
ERIC GORMAN *Guard*
KEVIN LAWLESS *Fireman*
PADDY O'DONNELL *Porter*
WEBB OVERLANDER *Railroad station chief*
HANK WORDEN *Boxing trainer in flashback sequence*
PATRICK WAYNE, ANTONIA WAYNE,
MELINDA WAYNE, MICHAEL WAYNE,
ELIZABETH JONES *The Widow Tillane's tiny Maid*
HARRY TYLER *Pat Cohan*
DON HATSWELL *Guppy*
PHILIP STAINTON *Anglican bishop*

INTRODUCTION

My fascination with this wonderful movie goes way back to the local cinema in the Ayrshire holiday-town of Girvan in 1952, the year the film went on general release, when I was four and a half years of age. Little did I know then that, some 40 years on and after a long series of coincidences involving *The Quiet Man*, I would be writing this book. And little can those who fashioned this classic have realised all those years ago that it would have such enduring qualities. I can reveal, for instance, courtesy of Video Collection International, that, on being launched as a video presentation in October 1985, 33 years after its release in the cinema, *The Quiet Man* sold an incredible 195,275 copies within the first four years in Britain alone, despite being shown regularly on television. By early 1990 the figures were nudging a quarter of a million and there are no signs of the film's popularity waning. It is a John Ford masterpiece which won two Oscars in 1952 when faced with competition from Fred Zinnemann's *High Noon*, Cecil B. De Mille's *The Greatest Show On Earth* and a host of other challengers. It has become a collectors' item and is now very much a cult movie. No other feature film has sold anywhere near as much in recent years and at one stage it doubled sales of the nearest title, remarkable figures which are a tribute to the movie's greatness.

These statistics came to light in one of the aforementioned co-incidences to affect me over the years in terms of this film. During a business lunch held at Hampden Park, the very cradle of Scottish football, by sheer chance I found myself sitting next to a delightful Irishman from Limerick, Paddy Toomey. It transpired he was the director and general manager of Video Collection International who had bought the rights to the movie. A few months earlier, when researching this book, I had noted his company's name on the video cover of *The Quiet Man* and, when I mentioned this, he related these amazing sales figures, figures which had staggered even a man of his wide experience in the business. In a letter a few weeks later he informed me that the sales took *The Quiet Man* into the all-time top five video sellers of feature films in the UK. Here is a breakdown on the video launched on 1 October 1985 and sold at a retail price of £7.99 as part of a package of 50 titles: *1985–86* 57,350, *1986–87* 40,780, *1987–88* 23,750, *1988–89* 12,660 *Total:* 134,540. After being relaunched as the lead title on the Cinema Club label on 1 April 1989 it outsold the nearest title by two to one over the first four months and, within six months, by early September 1989 it had sold another 60,735 copies taking the total to 195,275! In addition, the film is also in great demand in America, Canada and Australia among the descendants of Irish immigrants. A couple of years ago a Spanish film crew from Barcelona arrived in Ireland to make a documentary about it. So pleased were the staff of Video Collection International with the rights coup pulled off by Paddy Toomey and the success it brought their company that they had his photograph superimposed on an action shot of John Wayne in the famous fight scene, with suitable subtitles – and it hangs proudly in Toomey's office.

Now back to that cinema outing in Girvan, a town which looks out across the sea to Ireland and Ailsa Craig, that great volcanic rock and bird sanctuary, probably better known to those who have sailed the short journey back and forth between the two countries as 'Paddy's Milestone'. As the crow flies, Girvan is little more than 250 miles from where *The Quiet Man* was filmed. And exactly a year after the cast had gone back to Hollywood it was on the screen in Scotland in glorious Technicolor. It was to be an evening of acute embarrassment for my mother, father and elder sister who had decided to give me a treat by taking me to the 'pictures', as they say in my native city of Glasgow. Apparently, much to the annoyance of the audience, I kept shouting out: 'When will we see this Quiet Man?', not quite appreciating all that was happening on the screen in front of me. Nevertheless, even all these years later I have a faint recollection of those cinema visits; my late father, Pat, taking me for a gourmet lunch of egg and chips in a little tea-room just around the corner from the cinema on another occasion and a wonderful, wise-cracking uncle, James, who would tease me by saying: 'Have you heard about the Quiet Man? He knocks the door with a sponge.' Happy days indeed.

Through the sixties and seventies I saw the film a number of times on television, usually around Christmas or Easter time. It is replete with Irish customs skilfully integrated into the plot by John Ford who lovingly pieced together every frame and it is one I really grew to appreciate and take great enjoyment from. On 13 July 1982 I returned to a deserted Glasgow home to experience another of those *Quiet Man* coincidences. My wife, Rosaleen, and daughters, Dara, Kathleen and little Rosaleen, were on holiday in Ireland. As chief sports writer, I had been covering the Spanish World Cup football finals for *The Daily Express* and, after six exhausting weeks on the roads to Malaga, Seville, Barcelona and Madrid, I was feeling tired and more than a little sorry for my lonely predicament. I switched on the kettle to make a cup of tea and flicked the television switch in the kitchen just as the delightful, opening music of *The Quiet Man* began. Within seconds I was sitting back, feet up and at peace with the world because of a film which for me has always summed up the endearing qualities of Ireland – even in modern times when, sadly, parts of that country have longed for peace and tranquillity.

My own connections with Ireland go back to the early fifties – those of my family go back much further – when I was taken on a couple of occasions for a holiday with relations near Fintona, County Tyrone. An old and dear aunt once told me that, had my ancestors not been forced to leave the area in a bit of a hurry, for reasons which are unclear, and changed the family name, I would have been an O'Neill (the name of the kings of Tyrone) born and bred in that province! So for me it was interesting to discover that in the late 1700s, after being accused of plotting against the British Crown, Robert Morrison, great-great-grandfather of John Wayne, fled the same Ireland in search of a new life in America where he became an elder in the Presbyterian Church and a brigadier-general in the Ohio militia during the war of 1812. John Ford's family also suffered similar problems, with some leaving the Galway area where he was to make parts of the film.

That first holiday in Tyrone had come at exactly the time *The Quiet Man* was being filmed on location a couple of hundred miles south-west, in the village of Cong, County Mayo, and surrounding area including Maam Valley and other parts of beautiful Connemara. Those early memories were happy ones as we stayed on the family farm at 'Aghafad' with Uncle John McBride and Aunt Kate. I got into terrible trouble for opening the gate to a field and allowing the horse to gallop off down the road, for opening a door and letting dozens of piglets take off in as many directions, and for terrorising the chickens and geese! We went to church on a Sunday courtesy of the horse and trap, thankfully reunited once again, and the first week I made the miscalculation of stepping aboard before Aunt Kate. It was nothing to do with a lack of manners but rather the fact that she was not quite in the light-weight class. The trap pitched violently to one side as she climbed aboard and to a nipper like myself it was a frightening experience. The following week I was cute enough to hide behind the kitchen door and wait till I knew for certain she was on board before venturing outside. In a way, and without appreciating it, I was very much in a *Quiet Man* environment. The set-up, with its white-washed cottage and outbuildings, was just like White O' Mornin', the old cottage used in the film, as was the happy, carefree way of life. It was to be 20 years before I would return to the Emerald Isle – a summer holiday with friends in the town of sweet Dungloe, County Donegal in 1971. Indeed, it was there, a couple of years later in 1973, that my wife-to-be and I really began, as they say in the movie, 'walking out together'. She had been born in nearby Gweedore but was also on holiday from Glasgow where her family had moved that same summer of 1951 when *The Quiet Man* was being filmed. The rest, as they say, is history. We became engaged that Christmas Eve and were married in June the following year and one of the first things we did was build a white-washed cottage in Gweedore where, over the years, we have spent as much time as possible.

It was during one of those breaks, in Easter 1985, that I decided I must make an effort to find out where *The Quiet Man* had been filmed and visit the area. My inquiries were a bit rushed and we set off to tour the west coast of Ireland none the wiser. The notion had completely gone out of my head by around the third day and there we were driving along in Connemara at a fair speed when I hit the brakes and put the car into reverse. No, I hadn't been seeing things! There it was, at the side of the road in the middle

The little bridge used for the scene at the beginning of the film. It is actually on the Galway–Clifden Road

of nowhere, a small green-and-white sign proclaiming 'Quiet Man Film'. We turned off the main road on to a track leading to the little hump-back bridge used in the opening scenes as Michaeleen Oge Flynn stops the horse and trap to allow Sean Thornton a look at the old Thornton cottage. We looked around for any other landmarks without success before continuing our journey. That *Quiet Man* sign no longer exists, as I discovered on a subsequent journey during the research of this book, but the bridge can be found just off the Galway-Clifden road a few miles before Maam Cross. A green sign pointing left and advertising 'Connemara Country Club (Cottages)' leads on to the instantly recognisable location.

That lucky find was to be it for another three years till the summer of 1988 and a chance meeting in the Spanish Costa del Sol holiday resort of Benalmadena near Malaga. We met a couple from Hamilton, Lanarkshire, Stevie and Mary Donnelly, in our hotel bar and talked over a few drinks. One of the topics of conversation was films and Stevie said there was one particular movie he was crazy about. Before he said another word I inquired: '*The Quiet Man?*' He just about fell off his seat at what had been

Barry Fitzgerald stamp

an inspired guess. He and some friends, it transpired, had set up a *Quiet Man* appreciation society some years earlier and held occasional quiz nights on the film in his public house. Not only was he able to tell us that the movie had been shot in Cong and the grounds of fabulous Ashford Castle on the outskirts of the village, but he had actually been there! He proved to be a real fund of information and even had access to a rare copy of Maurice Walsh's *Green Rushes* on which director John Ford based his classic. And as if to prove his point even more, Stevie reached into his wallet and produced a special postage stamp bearing the impish features of Barry Fitzgerald. It was virtually there and then that I decided this book, which had been in the back of my mind for a number of years, must be written. Since that holiday meeting the Donnellys have become good friends, our respective children keep in touch, and they have been guests at our own White O' Mornin' in Donegal.

The following Easter, 1989, boosted by that meeting in Spain, I visited Cong to begin my research on this story and called in at Jack Murphy's small general store. Above it is a rather misleading, but instantly recognisable, sign proclaiming 'Pat Cohan – Bar'. It was outside the door that the famous fight sequence between Sean Thornton and Red Will Danaher reached its climax. It is the starting point for anyone on the trail of *The Quiet Man* and Jack Murphy, who took part as a young extra in 1951, sells for just one Irish punt an informative booklet on the film, Cong itself and the surrounding area. As I spoke to him a couple from America wandered in looking for information about the film and told him they had it on video back in Cincinnati. Like all others who visit the shop they admired the old black-and-white photographs which were taken by some of the locals at the time from behind the movie cameras and which have become as treasured as the gold- and jewel-encrusted 12th-century Processional Cross of Cong, acknowledged to be one of the finest works of art of the period in Europe. The folks from Cincinnati then went off to the local post office in search of one of those commemorative Barry Fitzgerald stamps from postmistress Mary Gibbons who manned the overworked village switchboard during those heady days of filming.

With my wife and family I stayed at Ashford Castle where John Wayne, Maureen O'Hara and the other stars had lived while on location. I interviewed the warm, very helpful, local people including the stand-ins for Wayne and O'Hara and those who were extras. Lord Killanin, a wonderful, charming man, was also a great source of information and inspiration. The former President of the International Olympic Committee was a great friend of John Ford through family ties and acted as a consultant to him on *The Quiet Man*. So, armed with new information, I visited all of the location sites used in a film which, 40 years on, is rightly hailed as a classic. At last I was off and running on a project which had, in a strange kind of way, been stalking me for most of my life.

And now the pages ahead take us in the footsteps of *The Quiet Man*.

Chapter One
GREEN RUSHES

As *The Quiet Man* flickers to life, the very first names to appear on screen, superimposed on the fairy-tale backdrop of Ashford Castle and Lough Corrib with its hundreds of islands, bays and coves in County Mayo, give no clue to the drama and in-fighting which went on behind the scenes before, during and after the making of the film. The story behind the story carries as much intrigue as the actual movie itself. Because of an incredible chain of events it would take director John Ford 15 long years to attain his cherished dream but as Father Peter Lonergan, parish priest, says as the train pulls into Castletown: 'Well then now, I'll begin at the beginning.'

The movie's plot is simple but intriguing. Sean Thornton (John Wayne) returns to his native Ireland having spent most of his life in America where he worked in the steel mills and had been a professional boxer. After accidentally killing an opponent in the ring he decides on the peaceful Innisfree as the place to rebuild his life. However, life turns out to be anything but tranquil. He quickly meets and falls in love with a wild red-head, Mary Kate Danaher (Maureen O'Hara) but encounters her intransigent brother Red Will (Victor McLaglen) who is incensed that the returned Yank has bought back the old Thornton land and cottage from the Widow Tillane (Mildred Natwick). Danaher had designs on the land and still has designs on the widow. It is only when the other main characters, including the priest and the minister, lead Danaher on in terms of his chances with the widow that he gives his consent to the marriage of his sister and Thornton. When Danaher discovers the deception during the celebrations after Mary Kate's wedding, he flattens Thornton and refuses to hand over the agreed dowry. While neither the custom nor the money matter to Thornton, Mary Kate reckons she is not properly wed without them and, using the ultimate female weapon, says she will cook and sew – but nothing else! After much drama – plus plenty of humour from the likes of Michaeleen Oge Flynn (Barry Fitzgerald), Fr. Lonergan (Ward Bond), Feeney (Jack McGowran) and a host of other characters – Thornton blows his stack, drags his runaway wife through fields, demands the dowry and takes on Danaher in arguably the cinema's most famous fight. But, like all good fairy tales, the film has a happy ending.

However, before naming the stars, John Wayne, Maureen O'Hara and Barry Fitzgerald, the opening titles proclaim: 'A Republic Production. Herbert J. Yates presents — John Ford and Merian C. Cooper's Argosy Production.' Republic had been founded in 1935 and just two years earlier Ford's attention had been attracted by a Maurice Walsh story, *The Quiet Man*, which had appeared in a publication called the *Saturday Evening Post*. It was a short story about Shawn Kelvin who, at the age of 20, had left his native Ireland and gone to work in the slag heaps of Pittsburg, USA, where he became a professional boxer. Fifteen years later he returns home looking for an Eden and an Eve. He buys a small farm and tries to shut out the unhappy memories of America. Shawn begins courting the lovely Ellen O'Grady but her elder brother and guardian, big Liam, hates Shawn and refuses to pay the dowry for his sister. Shawn and Ellen go ahead and get married but the new wife insists that he fights for her honour and the dowry.

Maurice Walsh had based his main character, who would be played by John Wayne, on a 17-year-old lad called Paddy whom his father had hired as a farm help, a lad who loyally stayed with the family all of his life and would carry John Walsh into church when he became an old man struggling to walk. The real Paddy Bawn and the eventual character played by John Wayne in *The Quiet Man* bore no resemblance except for their quality of steadfastness. He was no boxer although he was known to have the odd fight when he had a drink or two inside him. It was a tribute from Walsh to a lifelong friend and, after the movie was released in 1952, Paddy became a local legend and revelled in his new-found fame.

By the time Ford bought the rights to the story on 25 February 1936, for a mere $10, Walsh had expanded it and incorporated it in a best-selling book, *Green Rushes*. *The Quiet Man* was part three of a five-part story centred on a rural community around 1920 as the Black-and-Tan war flared up in a mountainous region of south-west Ireland. It begins with Paddy Bawn Enright (Shawn Kelvin, in the earlier, shorter version), a lad of 17, leaving Ireland for America to seek his fortune then returning to his native Kerry, a quiet man not wishing to talk of himself or his deeds when abroad. He had worked in the glare of the open-hearth steel furnace in Pittsburg and had been a sparring partner at a boxing camp in New York State. He is 32 when he returns home hoping to end his days in 'a quiet place on a hillside' but finds the old Enright land has been bought up 'meanly' and added to the acres of Red Will O'Danaher, a huge, raw-boned man with the strength of an ox, overbearing and given to berserk rages (Big Liam in the original tale). Paddy Bawn does nothing about it and is ridiculed by the locals, who reckon no real Irishman would take the loss of his land quietly. He purchases a small croft, a four-roomed, lime-white, thatched cottage on a warm shelf of land on Knockanore Hill commanding the best view in all Kerry and looking out between the black portals on the River Shannon. Knockanore is heaven to him but he is drawn into the IRA flying column in the fight against English rule. In this version Mickeen Oge Flynn (Michaeleen in the movie) is second in command of an IRA flying column and described as an unconditional republican who is celibate by inclination and half-priest by training. Hugh Forbes is an ex-British officer and leader of the flying column and Sean Glynn a gentleman farmer and IRA intelligence officer. Matt Tobin is a thresher who worked a Thomson gun with Paddy Bawn in many an ambush against the Tans. Paddy has no plans to take a wife but on Sundays he goes to the old grey chapel and, after a time, his eyes begin to fix themselves on a red-haired girl two rows in front of him. Her name is Ellen Roe O'Danaher (Ellen O'Grady in the original version), the 30-year-old sister of Red Will. Her brother keeps men away from her and uses her as a housekeeper at his Moyvalla ranch farm. Red Will himself is not the marrying kind until his neighbour dies and he sends an accredited emissary to open negotiations with the widow. She, however, refuses to 'come wife to a house with another woman at the fire corner'. That is the line Ford was to seize upon years later to introduce his plot to the movie.

A happy off-screen chat between the stars, in Ashford Farmyard

As *Green Rushes* continues – the title originates from the old Gaelic love-saying which, translated, is: 'I will spread green rushes under her feet that she may step softly', (it was customary to spread rushes on the stone floors of cottages if company was expected) – O'Danaher actually seeks out Paddy Bawn and offers him Ellen's hand in marriage. He invites Paddy to Tade Sullivan's bar but it's Paddy who has to buy the drinks! O'Danaher offers a dowry of £100 at the end of harvest, 'if prices improve'. The marriage goes ahead but the widow doesn't wait for Red Will and marries her cattleman. O'Danaher now adds a real dislike to the contempt he has for Paddy Bawn. However, Paddy and Ellen settle down well and he buys a horse and cart to take them to Listowel on market days. All is bliss till Ellen insists on Paddy getting her fortune from Red Will. After several fruitless attempts to secure the dowry the big fight is on, with Mickeen Oge Flynn taking bets.

The fisticuffs begin among cone-pointed corn-stacks on O'Danaher land, with Matt Tobin's threshing machine going at full steam and a crowd of 'not less than two-score men' around. Red Will looks in the direction of Flynn and Glynn and inquires: 'Is the IRA in this too?' Flynn thinks: 'If the IRA were in this, not even the desolation of desolation would be as desolate as Moyvalla.' Red Will refuses to pay, Paddy says: 'That breaks all bargains,' and gives him back his sister. 'You can't do that,' fumes Red Will. 'It's done,' says Paddy Bawn. Aware of sly laughter and derision, Red Will hands over a wad of crumpled banknotes and screams: 'Here's your money. Take it – and what's coming to you! Take it! Count it. If ever I see your face again I will drive that through it,' showing a fist. 'Count it, you spawn.' Paddy Bawn heads for the face of the engine and Ellen Roe, who has witnessed the full scene, runs over and opens the door of the firebox, scorching her hand on the hot bar. Charred paper floats out of the funnel top and Red Will, in a fury, tries to attack. But the first punch, a right-hook from Paddy Bawn, lifts the 200-pound O'Danaher right off the ground and, in the space of five minutes, the man known in America as Tiger Enright (Trooper Thornton in the movie), sends O'Danaher to the ground eight times without his adversary landing a punch. Ellen Roe takes her man's arm and goes with him, 'proud as the morning', but insists on the last word: 'Mother o' God, the trouble I had to make a man of him!'

Green Rushes

John Ford loved the story and it became his most cherished possession. When he found such a jewel he would brood over it and incubate it for as long as necessary. When the time came, he would expand it into a novella and play about with the names of the main characters; Paddy Bawn Enright would become Sean Thornton, a mixture of his own real first name and the surname of his cousins from his beloved Spiddal area in Galway; Feeney, his own surname, would be given to Jack McGowran, playing the lackey of Red Will Danaher. But with *The Quiet Man* Ford's patience was to be tested to the limit.

Chapter Two
THE BATTLE FOR *THE QUIET MAN*

Republic Pictures was still a fledgling organisation when it signed up John Wayne almost immediately after his early stints at studios such as Columbia, Warner Brothers, Paramount and Mascot. The latter had been run by Nat Levine very much with an eye on the dollar. He was more interested in the quantity of box-office cash than the quality of films he produced. A company called Consolidated Film Laboratories had Mascot as a client and had already taken over Majestic Pictures.

Now enter Herbert J. Yates, head of Consolidated, ex-Wall Street financier and entrepreneur who had been awaiting the main chance to break into the movie business in terms of lucrative production and distribution. If Levine had a bad reputation in the money stakes, he couldn't hold a candle to Yates who had the soul of an accountant rather than a movie showman and who was only interested in making 'sure things' in a movie sense; years later he would be accused by Ford and Cooper of dipping his fingers in the *Quiet Man* till. He had ruthlessly foreclosed on Mascot and two other companies, merged their best talents, and founded the independent Republic Pictures in the San Fernando Valley in 1935 where, for the next 25 years, they would produce a conveyor belt of westerns, serials, musicals and all-action films. Many were B-movies and made in less than a week for just $10,000, but the quality improved as Yates contracted Wayne to a certain number of pictures a year. So watertight was the contract that even when war broke out a number of years later, and despite the fact Wayne's friends and colleagues like Ronald Reagan, Clark Gable, James

Stewart and John Ford had enlisted, Yates still wouldn't let him join up and threatened to sue if he walked out. The same Yates was not, however, averse to leasing him out to other studios for a fat fee. What an irony that John Wayne, who fought every battle imaginable on celluloid, never sampled the real thing.

John Ford later had production deals with Yates but never worked for him on an exclusive basis because he neither liked nor trusted the czar of Republic. And because Ford had retained his professional freedom, it allowed him to shoot a film he had long wanted to make, *The Informer*, like *The Quiet Man* a story set in his native Ireland. *The Informer* had been turned down by Fox, Warner Brothers, Paramount, Columbia and MGM yet it was to go on and win four Oscars including one for Ford and one for Victor McLaglen. It had, in fact, been one of the smaller studios in Hollywood, RKO Radio, which had shown faith in Ford and the movie. Now enter Merian C. Cooper, who was second in command to David O. Selznick at RKO and a real southern gentleman. The studio had changed hands a few times in the thirties and 1934 proved no exception. Among its financial backers were Howard Hughes and Joseph P. Kennedy, father of John Fitzgerald Kennedy who was to be of great political interest to Ford a generation later because of their mutual Irish-Catholic backgrounds. (In fact, Ford was to shut down filming on *Cheyenne Autumn* for two days when President Kennedy was assassinated in Dallas, Texas, on 22 November 1963. He led the cast and crew in The Lord's Prayer, sang the 'Battle Hymn of the Republic' and had a bugler sound taps.) Unfortunately, Joe Kennedy sold-out right in the middle of *The Informer* but Ford, backed by Merian Cooper, was allowed to complete it and draw from Victor McLaglen one of his greatest performances. Ford literally bullied him to an Oscar-winning performance as Gypo Nolan. McLaglen was a prime target for the director's badgering tactics. It is said that Ford told others to get the actor drunk before some of the most important scenes and then put him through hell the next day on set, provoking him to bring out his best. It has also been suggested that Ford kept McLaglen drunk, or suffering from a hangover, for three whole weeks so as to capture the groping confusion of Gypo Nolan on screen. Lord Killanin, Ford's friend, comments later on this rather extreme technique.

While *The Quiet Man* would allow Ford to indulge in the Hollywood interpretation of a romantic, pastoral Ireland in the shape of a poetic comedy, a fairy tale, it was the dark side of the moon in term's of that country's political turbulence – The Troubles as they are known – that he tackled in *The Informer*. As will be seen later, Ireland was inextricably linked to just about everything Ford did. He delighted in telling friends that he came from 'a family of peasants'. But while Ford enjoyed his successes he simply couldn't find a studio to accept his dearest project.

He had in mind to play Mary Danaher, his female lead in *The Quiet Man*, the Irish actress, Maureen O'Hara, and in 1944 went to see her. She recalled in an interview on Gay Byrne's *The Late, Late Show* beamed from RTE in Dublin:

> I was making a movie and one day John Ford came to the studio to see me about *The Quiet Man*. He was reputed not to like wearing fancy clothes and he would always have white flannels and a dark navy jacket. When his wife would buy him new clothes he would burn holes in them so they would look old. He always looked a bit disreputable and he wore an old felt hat which my father had sold him in Woodrow's shop in Dublin.
>
> The day he arrived there was a new, young policeman on duty and he thought this dreadful-looking, disreputable man could have no reason to be in the studio and wouldn't let him in. The number two studio man at RKO at that time was called Joseph Nolan who came down to the set to see me and said: 'Mother of God, John Ford came to see you and they wouldn't let him into the studio. What are we going to do? He's furious. Please call him, calm him down and ask him to come back tomorrow and we'll put out the red carpet.' So I called John Ford, who was a wonderful man, and the idea of the red carpet really appealed to him. He came back the next day and they really did put out the red carpet. He had come to see me for a handshake contract to make *The Quiet Man* as soon as he could raise the money. He also had handshake contracts with John Wayne, Barry Fitzgerald and Victor McLaglen.

Just a final adjustment to Maureen O'Hara's make-up

Apart from studios not believing the movie was a money-making project, one of Ford's main problems over the years had been that *The Quiet Man* story line lacked real depth. It was more a written piece than a plot, thick with the type of characters required for a movie and that seems to have been one of the reasons so many studios had turned away from it. Ford had decided that it must be shot on the west coast of Ireland, close to those family roots of his. It would also be very expensive because he insisted on Technicolor. Eventually, in March 1946, Ford and Merian C. Cooper, who had developed a great mutual respect over the years, decided to bring to fruition an old ambition to form their own film production company. So Argosy Productions was born, with Cooper as president and financial controller and Ford, chairman. Both men were creative forces with strong motion-picture backgrounds. Now, surely, Ford's dream of making *The Quiet Man* would become reality. The battle intensified to raise the cash and the letters and telegrams were soon under way.

The first letter was to Ford's friend, Lord Killanin, in Ireland, a man who had an interest in film-making and who later was to spring to international recognition as head of the Olympic Movement.

11 July 1946: Dear Michael, Despite the fact we have a Labour government in England and the entire world is leaning towards the left, I am still feudal enough to be happy that your line will go on. I am planning to do a picture for Alex Korda next summer. It is a story by Maurice Walsh called 'The Quiet Man' and, honestly, I think it is a grand story. Alex, I believe, is going to approach you with the possibility of you working on it. It might be fun. We will wander around shooting it in colour all over Ireland but with the stress laid on Spiddal. I will bring the principals from America and pick up the incidental parts and bits in England and Ireland. As I said before, it will be photographed in Technicolor and should be beautiful. I'm glad you came out of the war with no ill effects. I'm dictating this now from a hospital cot [Ford mentioned some illness or injury in most of his letters] as I have just been operated on for a slight injury received. I am fine, not much pain despite the fact I was operated on yesterday. I expect to be out in four or five days. Affection, Jack.

1946 undated – Lord Killanin to Sir Alexander Korda, chairman of London Film Productions Limited, who has indicated he will fund the movie: Dear Sir Alexander, I've had a letter from Jack Ford about the making of Maurice Walsh's The Quiet Man over here next year. It appears from Jack's letter that my help in the film might be of some use.

9 August 1946 – Ford to Killanin: Dear Michael, Thanks for your note. I think we can have a lot of fun on 'The Quiet Man'. It's a lovely story and I think we should go all over Ireland and get a bit of scenery here and a bit of scenery there and really make the thing a beautiful travelogue besides a really charming story. I intend to bring Mary and Barbara [his wife and daughter] with me so you had better tell my cousin Michael Connolly, across the bridge at the foot of the Buirin to get the jaunting car out as they will probably want

SIXTY EIGHT SIXTY ODIN STREET
HOLLYWOOD, CALIFORNIA

August 9th, 1946.

Dear Michael:

　　　　　Thanks for your note. I think we could
have a lot of fun on "The Quiet Man". It's a lovely
story and I think we should go all over Ireland and get
a bit of scenery here and a bit of scenery there and
really make the thing a beautiful travelogue, besides
a really charming story. I intend to bring Mary and
Barbara with me so you had better tell my cousin Michael
Connelly, across the bridge at the foot of the Búirín
to get the jaunting car out, as they will probably want
to see the country, even as far as Kylmore..where on
a clear day you can see Oliver Gogarty(God help you
this day, says the poor man in Dublin﹚.I just saw
Oliver St. John Gogarty through glass.)

　　　　　I have wi...
he will ...

Argosy Pictures Corporation

John Ford, ...
Merian C. Cooper, ...

September 29th, 1952.

Dear Michael:

　　　　　As usual, Brian is probably procrastinating,
although he promised me faithfully he would turn over a new leaf
(starting at the bottom of the page). I think we should protect
ourselves and consider doing "Bad Town Dublin", by Maurice Walsh
as a possibility. I don't advise making a decision now, but merely
to use it as a line of retreat, while like Monty, we are pivoting.

　　　　　"Bad Town Dublin" is a fascinating story with great
dramatic elements and outside the Dublin scenes it has some fine
possibilities for grand Irish 'scapes.

　　　　　Our plans here indicate that I'll disembark at
Shannon and drive straight on to Dublin...and after a couple of
days go to England. I'll wire you at both the Dublin and
Spiddal addresses. If you see Charles Fitzsimons, will you
advise him that we'll be coming through.

　　　　　Read "Bad Town Dublin" and give me your frank
opinion. I rather like it. However, I still think "Demi Gods"
is fascinating.

　　　　　My love to you, Sheila and the kids.

　　　　　　　　　　Jack

JF:S

The letters

to see the country . . . I have wired Alex Korda and I expect he will get in touch with you . . . On your next trip to Dublin you might get a copy of 'The Quiet Man'. It's in a volume called 'Green Rushes'. We here send you all much affection. Jack.

20 August 1946 – Ford to Killanin: Dear Michael, The story we consider doing is called 'The Quiet Man' by Maurice Walsh. It is a short story in a book called 'Green Rushes'. I am now convalescing on the Araner [his yacht] and I am gradually feeling better. Mary and Barbara are with me and both send their love to you and Sheila. Affection, Jack.

It is odd that Ford refers to *The Quiet Man* as though he is mentioning it to Killanin for the first time. And again he refers to his health.

28 August 1946 – Korda to Killanin: Dear Lord Killanin, Jack Ford is going to make here 'The Quiet Man' next year. That is sort of verbally agreed between himself, his partner, Merian Cooper, and myself, although no contract has been signed as yet. He told me he would like to have you co-opted on to the film but apart from his wish to co-opt you I would very much like to have a talk with you when you come over here in October. Would you let me know when you will arrive. You can find me either at this office or at Claridges Hotel. Please give my kindest regards to Lady Killanin. Yours sincerely, Alexander Korda.

1946 undated – Killanin to Ford: My Dear Jack, As you may have heard by now, for I think he is with you, I saw Alex Korda in London. He told me what sort of thing you want me to do in the way of liaison, making arrangements etc. I shall be delighted to do it if it fits in with both our plans. A.K. told me that there were no contracts signed although I see Maureen O'Hara mentioned herself, Wayne and McLaglen at a Press interview in Dublin. Perhaps you'll let me know as soon as anything is firm so that I can make arrangements and try to fit it in with my plans. What I am most anxious to know is details of what you require before your arrival and perhaps a note about the terms! Sheila is very well and we hope for an heir or heiress at the end of January. We shall go up to Dublin for that event.

30 January 1947 – Ford to Killanin on Argosy Pictures Corporation paper: Dear Michael, At long last, to quote the late Hanoverian, I am answering your letter. I am here in the wilds of Mexico directing a picture and believe me when I say it has been very, very difficult. One of the reasons that I have not answered sooner is that our contract with Korda is more or less up in the air. He and Cooper are still arguing about money, percentages, credits and what not, all of which is none of my business but it does concern me and my plans greatly. Cooper flew to Los Angeles yesterday to confer with Alex so we should have a decision shortly. My own belief is that we shall not do the picture until the summer of next year. I'm afraid it's too late now for the boys to get together. I hope that our plans will still work out. As far as money is concerned I am sure there will be no trouble and we will be asking a great deal from you. In other words you will have to go to work! I'm still eagerly expecting the news of your heir. I hope by the time this reaches you that you and your lovely wife will be happy parents and that everything is well. I'm dictating this between scenes so I must hurry. I promise faithfully to write later when I have the pressure of work off my shoulders. All my best, Jack.

Another letter, undated, from Ford to Killanin apologises for not writing and states: 'I've been very busy all around the country lecturing to college idiots. Horrible! Beatnicks, Commies, etc. I'm afraid I was rather rude on occasion.'

8 December 1947 – Ford to Killanin: My dear Michael, My Sinn Fein heart gave a leap of joy about you working for the end of Partition especially because you are carrying on your civic duties as the head of a great line of Irishmen and Irishwomen. The picture is still up in the air but I still hope to make it in Ireland this summer. At least it is still on the books but as you know, money and production is so tied up here and costs are so excessive that I have to proceed cautiously. I am going to Mexico tomorrow on the boat to prepare a script and to do

a little fishing. The family will be with me and we expect
to spend Christmas together there. When I return I hope to
make a quick flying trip to Ireland and see you and more or
less prepare production if possible. We will require your aid
very much. I could not do it without your help and knowledge
of the country, the people, the customs, etc. A very Merry
Christmas to you and yours. We'll all be thinking about you.
Affection, Jack.

Alex Korda and Merian C. Cooper failed to reach their various
agreements and it was back to the drawing board for Ford and
his dream. But then Cooper thrashed out an agreement with
RKO – who had come to Ford's rescue for *The Informer* – and
the deal was that Argosy would make three films for Cooper's
old employers, sharing the costs and net profits, and that the
Ford-Cooper company would have full creative control. But in
the small print RKO insisted that only if the first picture was a
success at the box office could Ford go on to make *The Quiet
Man*. In the event, Ford's magic touch temporarily deserted him
and, after *The Fugitive* flopped in 1947, the dream seemed to be
over again as RKO cancelled *The Quiet Man* indefinitely.

Maureen O'Hara recalled: 'Each year we would hold the summer
open and each year there was no money and we couldn't make the
movie. The script was taken to Fox, RKO and Warner Brothers
and all the studios called it a silly, stupid little Irish story. "It'll
never make a penny, it'll never be any good," they said. And
the years slipped by. John Wayne and I used to go to the studio
and say: "Mr Ford, if you don't hurry up I'll have to play the
widow-woman and Duke will have to play Victor McLaglen's
role because we will be too old!"' In the event, Wayne would be
five days past his 44th birthday and O'Hara 31 when shooting got
under way in June 1951.

From 1947 till 1950 Ford made five classic westerns under the
Argosy banner, hoping for the success and cash which would take
him to Ireland. He directed *Three Godfathers* with six of those who
would become the *Quiet Man* team, *Fort Apache* with eight, *She
Wore a Yellow Ribbon* with eight and in 1950 *Wagonmaster* and
Rio Grande with nine of the team, including the first appearance
together of John Wayne and Maureen O'Hara. It was also the first
Republic-Argosy picture and brought Ford and Yates together for

what promised to be a stormy relationship – Yates the human cash register and Ford the creative genius, already winner of Oscars as best director for *The Informer* (1935), *The Grapes of Wrath* (1940) and *How Green Was My Valley* (1941), the latter starring O'Hara working with both Ford and Barry Fitzgerald for the first time.

John Wayne had been instrumental in Ford shooting *Rio Grande* for Yates who wanted the star to induce his director friend to make movies for Republic. Being locked in the earlier-mentioned contract to make so many B-movies a year, Wayne, having worked for better studios and made better pictures, knew Ford could vastly improve Republic's quality at a time when Yates wanted to go up-market. Yates was concerned about the inroads television was making into his type of picture. In the thirties, 75 million Americans a week went to the movies. By the mid-forties, that had risen to 100 million a week, a figure which would be halved by television in less than a decade. So Yates created a new structure as follows: 'Jubilee' pictures – westerns made in one week for $50,000; 'Anniversary' pictures – made in two weeks at a cost of between $175,000 and $200,000; 'Deluxe' – made in three weeks at $500,000; and 'Premier' – at $1.5 million, shot over three months.

Wayne took the bull by the horns and with Ford's blessing decided to show *The Quiet Man* script to 'Old Man Yates' as he called him. Recalled Maureen O'Hara: 'Mr Yates read the script and his reaction was the same as that of the other studios – a silly little story which would make no money. But with the chance to snag John Ford and Merian C. Cooper, the two top men in Hollywood, he was ready to gamble. "Very well," he said, "I will finance it on one condition – that you make a western first with the same cast, same director, same everybody, to finance and make up for the money I'll lose on *The Quiet Man*."'

During the filming of that western, *Rio Grande*, in the Utah deserts in the summer of 1950, the cast witnessed the comical sight and sound of Ford and his favourite actress O'Hara, heads together and conversing at a mile a minute in Irish Gaelic. Whatever they were saying seemed to do the trick because Ford produced a masterpiece cheaply and at speed which pleased Yates so much that, even before it went on general release, he surprisingly gave the director the go-ahead for Ireland and *The Quiet Man* to be filmed at last in the summer of 1951.

Ford took off for Ireland almost immediately and, after returning to the States following his early reconnaissance mission, he sent the following letters:

20 September 1950 – Ford to Lord and Lady Killanin (two letters on the one page): Dear Sheila, Thanks for your nice note. Allow me to say again how happy I was to see you and all those darling children. My trip to Ireland was the happiest vacation I've ever had and I have you to thank for most of it. You know, Sheila, you are a very charming and gracious person. Hasn't anyone told you? Again my affection, Jack.

Michael, it looks as though we can go in the spring. I'm for active duty for a few weeks but only for a few weeks it would appear. My aunt Julia, 93 years of age, who drinks cocktails, smokes and drives her own car (you met her by the way), tells me that our location in Mayo is near the parish of Dunfeeney from which the Feeneys [Ford's ancestors] were driven in days gone by. Does it still exist? Affection, Jack.

30 March 1951 – Ford to Killanin: Dear Michael, Your letter of 8 March just received thank you. I was particularly happy about the possibility of you and Sheila having twins. I'll pray that all goes well as I know it will. God bless you all. I envy you your trip to Geneva, Rome and Naples. My own trip was rather interesting and yet depressing. I've been hospitalized since I came back with a double hernia operation. [He was shooting a documentary for the US Navy.] Too many hours in the air catapulting and landing on carriers, helicopters and especially climbing mountains. I've never climbed so many damned mountains in my life. However I'm bright-eyed and bushy-tailed at the moment and working hard. I am sending this by the hand of my business and unit manager, Lee Lukather, who is a wonderful guy. I wish you would brief him and help him on Ireland. You'll find him the most courteous Yank and most efficient. He is our advance man, the sort of guy who goes along with the mine detector. Mary and the family join me in their respects. I'll be pleased if you notify me of the event. As always, affection, Jack.

The following month, April 1951, Ford and master movie-cinematographer Winton Hoch, flew to Ireland to join Lukather and work out final details for shooting the picture. This also gave Ford the chance to visit properly the family home in Spiddal for the first time in 30 years. He had never been more emotionally ready to make his dream movie.

Chapter Three
THE CAST

Maurice Walsh

The great steamships plied their trade in human cargo stopping briefly in Ireland at Larne in Co. Antrim on the way from the west of Scotland to America. Six guineas bought a one-way ticket to a new life. The year was 1879 and, on 21 April, Maurice Walsh, whose life would be heavily influenced by all three of those countries and who would become a Customs and Excise officer, a whisky connoisseur and great writer, was born in Ballydonoghue between Listowel and Ballybunnion in Co. Kerry. It was the type of village that, if a traveller blinked, he or she would miss it. The third child and first son of John and Elizabeth Buckley, Maurice Walsh loved his native Ireland, loathing everything the British Empire represented although never being anti-British as such. And, it would be this love, as well as that of his adopted Scottish Highlands, which would inspire his books – or 'yarns' as he was fond of calling them – years later.

Another influence was that of his father, a man steeped in legend, and the young Maurice would sit at his feet, listening to his stories and those of his friends. His mother, on the other hand, like most Irish mothers, hoped he would become a priest but in 1892, at the age of 13, he resisted Franciscan recruitment. In fact, his mother failed to make a priest out of any of her three sons although one daughter became a nun, Sister Gabriel, and was later to enjoy an unheard-of privilege thanks to Maurice's great talent – permission to leave Listowel Convent to watch *The*

Maurice Walsh

Quiet Man. 'Mossie', as he was affectionately called, was then, at his mother's insistence, trained for the Civil Service, which she reckoned was the next best thing to an ecclesiastical existence. He was not keen on this either but joined in July 1901 to please her and was immediately transfered to Limerick as an assistant revenue officer in the Customs and Excise.

However, in 1906, after postings in various places in Ireland, England and his beloved Scotland, he began writing to supplement his income and, in 1908, he had two stories published in the *Irish Emerald*. That same year he married a red-head, Caroline Begg. Eleventh out of 13 daughters in a Protestant household, she converted to Catholicism and they were married in the local Catholic church of her native Dufftown – a huge step indeed for a

Protestant lass to take at the time. Maurice was then posted back to Ireland and Co. Rosscommon but because Caroline was pregnant, she stayed behind with her mother. Her husband had left the instruction that, if they had a son, he was to be named John, after Maurice's father. A boy it was but, in a little conspiracy with Father George Shaw, the parish priest who had wed them, Caroline had the boy, the first of their three sons, baptised Maurice.

Maurice senior was a great Irish nationalist despite working for the British Customs and Excise. Like John Ford, he had a cousin who had organised the Ballydonoghue Company of Irish Volunteers in 1916 and who had been shot by the Black-and-Tans. In 1922 Maurice volunteered to return to Ireland for service in the administration of the new Irish Free State. Caroline was against the move and stayed on in Scotland with their young family while he found accomodation in Dublin, still a dangerous town during the civil war and probably inspiring the title for the fifth part of *Green Rushes, Bad Town Dublin*. Forced to remain indoors at night – the activities of snipers made the streets unsafe after dark – and missing his wife and family, he eased the boredom and loneliness by writing about his memories of the Scottish Highlands which resulted in his novel, *The Key Above the Door*.

By August 1923, peace had come to Dublin and he was joined by Caroline and the children at a time when his writing career was really taking off. At 44 he was in his most prolific period but still found time to help re-form the Irish Customs and Excise. By the age of 55 he had a growing international reputation. At last he had really 'made it' and was financially independent. *The Key Above the Door* sold well but brought him no real financial benefits because he had sold the rights to his publisher. However, *While Rivers Run* sold more than 5,500 copies in its first year, 1928, and another 28,000 copies over the next two years, and *The Small Dark Man*, published in 1930, sold 38,000 in just over a year.

His big breakthrough came in 1933, however, when he reached the lucrative American market with his short story, *The Quiet Man*. It appeared on 11 February in the *Saturday Evening Post* and brought him a payment of $2,000. The Walsh connection with America had begun through relatives in New York, the Kissanes, one of whom worked for the publishers Brandt and Brandt. Carl Brandt, a friend, tried to place Maurice's stories wherever he could, especially with the help of his brother, Erd Brandt, assistant editor at the *Saturday Evening Post*. Carl did a lot of editing on Maurice's stories to cut them down to the *Post's* required length, which did not always please the author. Yet it was lucrative. In 1933 he had earned only £450 whereas with Brandt and Brandt the following year his income was $6,000. With a pension of £376 per annum from the Customs and Excise and his books selling well at home and abroad, he retired early to a fine family home in Blackrock, Dublin, where he continued to write at his leisure.

Apart from the $10 John Ford paid Walsh for the story rights, he paid a further $2,500 plus agreed a cut of any sale to a movie company. Republic would later pay Ford $10,000 for the rights and Walsh made a total of $6,000 from the film – hardly a fortune for a movie which would be watched by many millions in the years ahead.

John Ford

Encapsulating the personality of John Ford was a task even his close friends found difficult. Perhaps Hollywood's Frank Capra, who idolised the greatest director of them all, came closest when he said: 'Ford cannot be pinned down or analysed. He is pure Ford – which means pure great. John is half-tyrant, half-revolutionary; half-saint, half-satan; half-possible, half-impossible; half-genius, half-Irish – but all director and all American.'

Born Sean Aloysius O'Feeney, or Fearna, in Portland, Maine, USA, on 1 February 1895, he was the 11th and last child in the family. His father, John Feeney, had been born in the village of Spiddal near Galway in Ireland just after the famine. Here the family lived in a cottage on the estates of the Morris family, who were later to be given the title of Lord Killanin. Ford's mother, Barbara Curran, was also born in that part of Ireland and was sent to America by her family while in her teens. As a youngster, Ford spent holidays with relatives in Spiddal and picked up some Gaelic.

He failed to gain entry to the Naval Academy at Annapolis, rejected because of his eyesight, but refusing to take 'no' for an answer, Ford attempted to gatecrash the First World War; he was thwarted by the Armistice before he could get himself into the Naval Flying Corps as a photographer. He then headed for Hollywood and, aptly, on St Patrick's Day 1920 he met Mary

Lord Killanin (left) and John Ford

McBryde Smith, a Scots-Irish Protestant from North Carolina and they were wed just three months later. She had served as a nurse at Annapolis and her family had a strong navy background.

In 1921, a year after he was married, Ford headed for Ireland where the IRA were embroiled in a bitter struggle with the Black-and-Tans. His intention was to join his cousins, the Thorntons, in the fight for freedom and Ford claimed years later that, after crossing by boat from Portland to Liverpool, he travelled on the same ship to Dublin as the patriot and freedom-fighter, Michael Collins, who was carrying peace proposals from Lloyd George. There was great hatred for the English after years of misrule. By the early twenties, at the exact time Ford journeyed to the land of his fathers, an astonishing 43 per cent of Irish-born men and women were living abroad, compared to an average of four per cent in most other European countries. There were more than a million in America, more than half a million on mainland

Britain, with others scattered in Australia, Canada, New Zealand and South Africa. The population in Ireland had dropped from around ten million, before the great famine of the 1840s, to around the three million mark. In Ford's native Galway, Gaelic speakers dropped from 98,523 to 80,238 between 1911 and 1926. In Mayo, where much of *The Quiet Man* would be filmed, the drop was from 88,601, to 63,514 during this time as the English influence grew and emigration bit deep.

With a number of his relations on the run and one of their homes torched by the Black-and-Tans, Ford returned to the States filled with a sense of injustice and decided his best contribution would be through fund-raising to help in the battle which would force the British out of Ireland. There was also his young and bewildered wife to be taken care of and, with debts mounting because of his absence, he quickly returned to film directing, a craft to which he had been introduced by his elder brother, Francis, another actor who would take part as the old, white-bearded character in *The Quiet Man*. They settled in a grey, stone-built house at 6860 Odin Street, Los Angeles, and a regular guest for Sunday afternoon drinks was an ageing Wyatt Earp who would visit from Pasadena where he had retired after hanging up his holster. No doubt he influenced Ford in the making of *My Darling Clementine*.

Having survived the Great Depression of the thirties Ford had the money to invest in one of the great loves of his life, a white two-masted yacht which he called the *Araner* after the inhabitants of the islands off the Galway coast. Its acquisition saw Ford become more involved in navy intelligence, another passion of his life. By 1939 he was a lieutenant-commander in the naval reserve and quite comfortable with his dual role in life. The sea and the navy, like film directing, were in the blood. At the outbreak of the Second World War, President Roosevelt set up a foreign intelligence agency, the Office of Strategic Services – OSS. For four years Ford worked in reconnaissance, shot excellent documentaries and received a citation for filming while under fire at Midway. He was decorated with the Purple Heart and Hollywood gave him a special Oscar. At the end of the war he was awarded the Legion of Merit for 'meritorious conduct and outstanding services' and authorised to wear the Combat V as Captain Ford. Later he was to achieve the rank of a two-star admiral.

Ford fiercely protected his private life and would say: 'The truth about my life is nobody's damned business but my own.' He was practically interview-proof and when asked once how he got to Hollywood, he tersely replied: 'By train.' When making known his opposition to the McCarthyite purges within the Directors' Guild in Hollywood, he prefaced his remarks by saying: 'My name is John Ford and I make westerns.' He enjoyed making brief, quirky remarks about himself. He expressed a liking for 'good people, simple people, people who go on doing their job in the middle of cheats and crooks', and a dislike of 'sex, obscenity and degeneration' in films. Of his many westerns he said: 'I'm interested by the folklore of the West . . . showing what really happened, almost a documentary,' and he loved 'fresh air, the wide open spaces, the mountains, the desert'. Of his work he said: 'I rehearse the cast carefully and use a minimum of dialogue. I believe movies are primarily pictures so I play them that way. Let the pictures do the talking for you . . . occasionally you get some luck in pictures. If something happens that wasn't premeditated, photograph it. . . . Someone called me the greatest poet of the western saga. I am not a poet, and I don't know what a western saga is. I would say that is horseshit. I'm just a hard-nosed, hard-working run-of-the-mill director.' (Lindsay Anderson *About John Ford*, 1981)

He was, of course, much, much more than that. A great admirer of Shakespeare, Ford could emulate that talent of mixing tragedy with farce. Knockabout comedy and tragedy co-existed with perfect ease in his work. No director ever ranged across the landscape of the American past as he did. He encompassed the worlds of Lincoln and Lee, Twain and O'Neill, the great wars, the western and trans-Atlantic migrations, the horseless Indians of the Mohawk Valley and the Sioux and Comanche cavalries, the Irish and Spanish incursions and many other moments of history. He developed his craft in the twenties, achieved dramatic force in the thirties, epic sweep in the forties and symbolic evocation in the fifties. Famed for his celtic and cavalry trilogies, he worked during the great years and right through the fifties, Hollywood's final decade as a living reality and probably its greatest for westerns and musicals. When it came to westerns, Ford was top gun. That proof came with the likes of *Stagecoach*, which he reckoned was worth an Oscar, and others like *She Wore a Yellow Ribbon* and *Fort*

Apache. Despite the fact his sight was not very good, he had the true eye of the film-maker: the surprising power of inner vision and the ability to edit as he looked through a lens.

Lord Killanin, who knew Ford in all of his moods, recalled:

> He was two different people depending on whether or not he was drinking. He was well educated having been to the University of Maine. He could also be quite irreverent towards his Catholic background and he had a deep suspicion of most clerics. In the days when I visited him in Odin Street his prized possession was an old Rolls Royce which he kept for many years and eventually made a lot of money from by renting it out. But he seemed fairly sceptical about others having big cars and when I accompanied him to Mass in Hollywood he would refer to the church as 'Our Lady of the Cadillacs'. Towards the end of his life he was always saying his rosary but in those days the beads hung over the top of the bed in Odin Street, then in the big house in Belair. But I should think the only time they were ever dusted then was when he moved house!

Lord Killanin

Lord Killanin is one of the most widely known Irishmen of his generation and has enjoyed a remarkable career embracing journalism, the army, film-making and sports administration.

Educated at Eton, the Sorbonne and Cambridge, he also holds honorary degrees from both parts of his divided country – the National University of Ireland and the University of Ulster. He came to international prominence as President of the International Olympic Committee from 1972 to 1980. His family name is Morris, in Irish MacMuiris or O'Muiris, with its derivation probably de Muiris from the French or Norman. This highly articulate man blessed with much humour and a down-to-earth attitude – his telephone number and address are in the Dublin phone book – looks on himself as Norman-Irish and, paradoxically, he is also a peer of the United Kingdom and a member of the House of Lords. His grandfather, a former Lord Chief Justice, was created a hereditary peer in 1900. Lord Killanin's family was Catholic with the result that, during the penal times of 1692–1829 when the British forbade Catholics to hold either land or high office, the name vanished from the history of Galway where the Morris family had resided since the 14th century. His grandfather and uncle both became Unionists, supporting the union between Ireland and Great Britain, but his father, killed in the First World War, had Nationalist tendencies.

In an interview at his atmospheric Dublin home, sitting in a study littered with mementoes – photographs of himself with Jimmy Carter in the Oval Office of the White House, with Leonid Brezhnev in the Kremlin and a host of other world leaders past and present, plus signed photographs from Elizabeth R and Yuri Gargarin, the first man in space – he reminisced:

> It all began around 1840 when my great-grandmother died of cholera in an epidemic during the famine. She had just given birth to a son, my great-uncle, Sir George Morris, who, because of her illness, had fostered him to the Feeneys, John Ford's family and predecessors, who had a cottage on the Morris estates. I suppose my first contact with films came when I worked in Fleet Street in the early thirties as a reporter. I wrote some scripts for film director, Brian Desmond Hurst, who was from Co. Down. Then I went out to China in 1937 to cover the Chinese–Japanese wars for the *Daily Mail* – I was 23 at the time and had no hesitation. Pembrooke-Stevens of the *Daily Telegraph* was killed out there, O'Dowd-Gallagher was the *Daily Express* man. I had begun my working life on the *Express* but was fired by Christiansen, the editor, for inaccuracy – I'd probably be promoted for such a thing in today's press world! When the fighting was over I decided I would like to come back through the United States so I cabled London to ask the foreign editor if I could spend a few days there. I got a reply saying 'yes' provided I went to Hollywood and Chicago. Not a mention of Washington you'll notice. Hollywood and Chicago meant films and crime according to the boys sitting back in London. That was their view of America. I didn't quite know what to do till I remembered this contact with John Ford who had always claimed to be a relation of mine because I had a great-great-uncle who populated the Spiddal area at a time when the family tree was not very accurate. So I cabled John and said: 'Your former wicked landlord will be passing through. Can you

help me.' I sailed the Pacific to Vancouver and went down to Los Angeles by train. John greeted me on the platform with a cable which read: 'The Lord passed through on the *Empress of Japan* safely.' He took me to Odin Street in the old Rolls-Royce and as he was not drinking at the time he got his brother-in-law, Wingate Smith, to show me around. I remember John showing me a copy of *Green Rushes* and saying: 'I want to make a film of that.' Little did I know that this story would lead to me meeting and befriending John Wayne.

John Wayne

He was the greatest box-office draw over a period of quarter of a century yet never legally changed his name to John Wayne. Born on 26 May 1907 in Winterset, Iowa, to Mary and Clyde Morrison just eight months after their wedding, they registered him on his birth certificate as Robert Michael Morrison, although a short time later they had a change of mind. Mary had one rich relation called Marion and, no doubt thinking she could secure a future inheritance for her son, she renamed him Marion Michael Morrison. There was to be no inheritance and perhaps it was with that story in mind that Wayne used a reference when he directed *The Alamo* many years later about being named after an uncle who 'didn't bequeath the farm'.

He was descended from a mixture of Irish, Scottish and English pioneers. Because of his father's ill health, the family moved to California where, in 1910, the movie industry had put down roots in Hollywood. A few years later, at the age of 11, he inherited a nickname which was to stay with him for life – Duke. Locals couldn't quite get used to calling a boy Marion and, because he did a paper round with his dog 'little Duke', he suddenly became 'big Duke'. Later, like his mentor John Ford, he was rejected for a place at the US Naval Academy in Annapolis. Instead he won a football scholarship to the University of California during which time his parents divorced, something he himself was to experience twice in later life.

It was through his USC football with the Trojans that his connections with the movies began. His coach, Howard Jones, got him a summer job at the Fox studios with the well-known western actor, Tom Mix, of whom John Ford was very fond. Wayne began moving props and other equipment from one set to another and it was one day during these menial tasks that he ended up on the set of *Mother Machree*, which Ford was directing, and landed a part as an extra, minding a flock of geese.

He actually got the chance to meet Ford and have a few words with him on their mutual love of football so that, in the autumn, he went back to college very much star-struck. The seeds of the movie business had been sown. A leg-break at football saw him quit university early and head back to Fox, looking for a permanent position at a time when films were becoming more and more popular with the advent of the talkies and jobs were plentiful. He worked on another couple of Ford movies as prop man and eventually proved to the director he was willing to take his chances as a stuntman. That brief role was enough for Ford to see that this young, raw talent had perhaps more to offer and, when he was preparing *Salute*, a story of sports' rivalry between the army and navy, to be filmed at the US Naval Academy, he asked Wayne to help hire experienced players who would be filmed in action sequences on the Annapolis playing-fields.

Both Ford and Wayne were at last into the Academy – but only as director and budding actor! Wayne went about his recruitment task but, just as they were about to leave Los Angeles, an uninvited guest appeared, complete with luggage – Wardell Bond. He and Wayne had been Trojan team-mates but disliked one another intensely. Wayne shouted that Bond was too ugly for films but the gate-crasher used his 200-odd pounds to push past his adversary. Ford nodded approval and Bond was in. By the time they arrived back in Los Angeles some months later they were the best of friends and calling Ford 'Coach' and 'Pappy'. (Bond had been born in Denver, Colorado, on 9 April 1903. *Salute*, completed in 1929, was his big break and he would go on to make something in the region of 200 movies.)

Meanwhile, the director, Raoul Walsh, who, like Ford years later, wore an eye patch, was casting *The Big Trail*. He was planning on having Gary Cooper or Tom Mix but money was tight and he decided to economise by using an unknown and Wayne, after being screen tested, was set for the star part of wagon-train scout. There was still, however, one stumbling block – his name. Walsh looked on Marion Morrison as a box-office disaster and said to him: 'How about Wayne, it has a nice ring to it.' The Duke didn't mind what they called him so long as he was a movie actor and promptly signed up for $75 a week. The film flopped financially and Fox declared bankruptcy. But Wayne was on his way and was snapped up by Columbia where he fell out with the boss. He moved on to Mascot Films then to the bigger Warner Brothers where he learned much more about his craft. And on 24 June 1933 he wed the first of his three wives, Josephine Saenz. Two years later he joined the fledgling Republic Pictures.

Victor McLaglen

While Wayne began his climb, an actor he had worked with in his first two movies, *Mother Machree* and *The Hangman's House*, was already established in the Ford stable. Victor McLaglen had experienced the life of an adventurer with a story few would believe. He was, without doubt, the most colourful of the *Quiet Man* cast in terms of the real world, never mind the world of celluloid. Amazingly, he brought out his autobiography, *Hollywood Express*, in 1934, the year before he won his Oscar in *The Informer* and with a great deal of his career still ahead of him. He described himself as 'a rolling stone' which chanced to defy the laws of nature and happened to gather some moss, and he described his book, long out of print, as 'the record of a man who was born lucky and found his luck in the oddest places'. He had to be persuaded into becoming a film actor, not because the life held no appeal for him but because it meant settling down in one spot and working for so many regular hours each day.

Born on 11 December 1886 in Tunbridge Wells, England, he was the eldest of eight sons and a daughter, his father, Andrew Charles Albert McLaglen being an Anglican clergyman who had taken the family to South Africa where he later became the Bishop of Claremont. The young McLaglen ran away from home and under age became a boy soldier during the time of the Boer War. Recalling his first day in the Life Guards at Knightsbridge Barracks in London he said: 'To find myself a recruit in a crack regiment thrilled me to the core and I was so overcome with emotion when I was sworn in that I could barely make the responses.'

It was after signing up that he showed an interest in boxing. As the Boer War drew to a close, McLaglen, who at 16 weighed in at

13 stones, was regimental heavyweight champion but he decided, under pressure from his father, to leave. However, he had also decided that the thrill of the professional ring was for him and he bought a boat ticket to Canada. There he worked on a farm, went down silver mines and then took up prospecting for gold. Mixed with all of these occupations was some boxing and even a bit of wrestling. Next he became a railway policeman at Owen Sound although boxing took over again in more ways than one and McLaglen spent a night in jail after becoming involved in an argument. The thrill of the ring grew greater and greater and he said of it: 'Frankly, I always liked a mixed reception. The knowledge that some of the fans were up against me always inspired me to do my very best. There is something primitive and thrilling in the sense that you are hammering against two opponents, the man opposite you in the ring and the peoples' choir outside it.'

On 26 December 1908 Jack Johnson became the first negro World Heavyweight Champion when he beat Tommy Burns in Sydney, Australia. Remarkably, his first fight after winning the title was against none other than Victor McLaglen on 10 March 1909 in Vancouver, British Colombia. It was not a title fight, with the result reported to be a 'no decision' after six rounds. In those days that indicated an exhibition bout. The Jack Johnson autobiography of 1927, *In the Ring and Out*, describes the fight as a 'minor ring affair' which he claims he won. He was certainly reported to have fought 'well within himself', but it shows just how highly-ranked McLaglen was when allowed into the same ring with the world champion. Ironically, the man who lost to Sean Thornton in *The Quiet Man* was the real pro in that scene!

McLaglen's record of the fight will interest boxing historians:

> One fight which should be recorded is the bout with Johnson just after he had captured the world title. For nearly 18 months I had been entrenching myself in the vanguard of America's heavyweights. The knowledge I was to fight the courageous negro, even though the bout naturally did not involve the title, thrilled me to the core and I toned myself up in double quick time, eager for the opening gong. Now there was at that time, a craze for what were rather stupidly called 'no decision' bouts. This freak of boxing history, which was an obvious offshoot

Victor McLaglen preparing to fight World Heavyweight Champion, Jack Johnson

of the official interference in the sport, implied that all fights ended in a draw, unless there happened to be a direct knock out . . . The fight took place in the Vancouver Athletic Club, which was crowded for the purpose and the fans were packed in like sardines, eager for their first glimpse of the famous world-beater. I recall that the great negro wore bright blue trunks and smiled that innocent smile of his all through the rounds. Men I have met, old boxers, have described Johnson as a disconcerting opponent.

He was frequently known, in his less important fights, to talk quite audibly to his opponent during the actual exchanges. His smile scarcely left his face, a child-like, good-natured grin, which lasted through the punches, regardless of their direction or their deliverer . . . I do remember how I tried my very best to rattle him during the last two rounds, conscious of the fistic immortality that would be mine were I lucky enough to slip a 'sleeper' . . . Johnson was undoubtedly the hardest man to hit whom I ever met. He was also the most charming opponent, standing well back and waving me forward when I slipped into the ropes in retreating before an attack of his . . .

During the first two rounds he had forced the pace, in a smiling, mechanical way, like a man who has a rush job of work to do and is anxious to get it over. Good luck and a certain ability to ship punishment without springing too serious a leak enabled me to weather the attack, and by the middle of the third round he had settled down to giving and taking fancy stuff. We both left the ring as fresh as we went into it. There had not been a single count, even from a slip. After towelling down we were photographed together, and neither of us had a mark to show for the fight. At this juncture it is only truthful for me to remark that I am the last man who would have expected the result to be similar had the title been at stake . . . He was certainly the greatest boxer I ever saw in action.

McLaglen, although he felt he could be listed with the best seven or eight heavyweights in America, knew he could settle for nothing less than being at the very top and he was honest enough to admit this would not happen. So he quit the serious ring and took part in one-night stands, taking on anything up to half a dozen opponents in one session. Again there was to be a change of direction and he sent a telegram back to his folks in England with the message: 'Joined a circus, feeling fine. Love, Victor.' Circus work took him all over British Colombia and Washington State but, after a couple of months, he walked out and became part of a vaudeville act!

In Nat Fleischer's *The Heavyweight Championship* of 1961 the author refers to Jess Willard, an ex-cowboy known as 'The Pottawatomie Giant' (Pottawatomie is in Kansas, Missouri), fighting McLaglen in a packed gymnasium in Springfield, also Missouri, in 1911. The admission fee to the fight, which Willard won, was 50 cents a head. At that stage McLaglen was known as 'The Great Romano', the biggest in a strongman act known as 'The Great Romanos', and he may well have been billed as such in the adverts for the fight. While the Johnson fight had been six rounds, it is not clear whether the Willard one was a knockout, had been stopped or was a points decision.

A boy soldier during the Boer War, a champion boxer, a vaudeville and circus act and just coming up for 28 years of age McLaglen was by now a real rolling stone and another new adventure lay around the corner – a trip to Australia. He then made his way across the South Seas where he signed on a pearling ship in Fiji for what was to prove a lengthy voyage. Seven days out the ship lost its main mast in a storm and then found itself becalmed, crippled and drifting. For almost a month McLaglen and his mates floated away from the shipping lanes, an experience he described as 'the most thrilling and frightening of my life'. Food ran out and things became grim as the 25-man crew went down with fever and water also ran out. They collected rain water in tarpaulins till thankfully another ship appeared on the horizon. McLaglen, safe and well, then headed off to India for eight months, followed by a spell of lion hunting in Africa! The outbreak of the First World War took him back on the first boat to England after he had experienced more than most could have crammed into two lifetimes and at the age of 28 he was attached to the Middlesex Regiment. He became impatient waiting to go to France and he switched to the Cheshires when he heard they were leaving imminently for Mesopotamia. 'When we took Baghdad,' he recalled, 'I was made Assistant Provost-Marshal of the city and my most serious task was to attempt to check the enemy espionage system behind our own lines.'

After the war, and no doubt with vaudeville and circus blood still coursing through his veins, he drifted into movies making his first film, entitled *The Call of the Road*, 'for fun'. It was a success. His size and expressive features made him ideal for the Hollywood silent movies of the twenties and, after making 20 films in England, he was taken to Tinseltown where his first film was aptly named *The Beloved Brute*, a title which was to become a personal billing for him in the years to come. In 1926 he and co-actor Edmund Lowe indulged in 'a fine exchange of Billingsgate' – using swear words – in the silent film *What Price Glory*, prompting a mountain of complaints to the studio from lip-readers! No fewer than five of his eight brothers were also film actors. When the youngest, Leopold, attempted to break into Hollywood in the mid-1930s, Victor showed no brotherly love by taking out a restraining injunction, he growled: 'There's only room for one McLaglen here!' Always the big, savage but soft-centred man of action who became a great favourite, and later friend, of John Ford, McLaglen had started off his movie career in England at £15 a week. His Hollywood contract at Fox gave him $1,000 a week for the first six months, $1,250 for the next six, $1,500 a week for the third six-month period and so on till he made $2,500 a week. He bought a house in Beverly Hills and had enough left over for a summer house in the hills outside Los Angeles. A move to Paramount saw him lift his earnings to $5,000 a week in the early thirties.

Maureen O'Hara

It was during those same thirties that a Dublin girl with flaming red hair and emerald-green eyes, who could have walked straight out of the pages of a Maurice Walsh story, began making her considerable mark on the movie industry. Born Maureen FitzSimons in Ranelagh, Dublin, on 17 August 1920, her father was in the clothing business and her mother had been an actress and singer. She would be given the stage name, Maureen O'Hara, by the legendary Charles Laughton and become the Queen of Technicolor.

The young Maureen first performed in public reading a short poem during the interval of a school play and, at her mother's

*Maureen O'Hara relaxes between scenes with a local book by Richard Hayward,
writer of 'The Humour is On Me Now', a song in the movie*

instigation, she studied at Burke's School of Elocution. Her first professional appearance came at the age of 12 on radio and then she studied music and dancing, appearing regularly in the chorus of the Dublin Operatic Society and in amateur productions. At 14 she joined the Abbey Theatre School and two years later she won the Coveted Dublin Feis Award for her performance as Portia in *The Merchant of Venice*. She was the youngest student ever to complete the Guildhall School of Music's drama course and, six months later, she received a degree from the London College of Music. At 17, after small roles, the Abbey Theatre offered her a leading part but a chance meeting with a prominent film figure in London led to a screen test there. In 1938, after two minor appearances in British films, *My Irish Molly* and *Kicking the Moon Around*, war clouds gathered causing uncertainty everywhere including the movie industry.

However, during her short time in London she had become the protégé of Charles Laughton. He saw a brief cut from one of her scenes and offered her a contract with Mayflower Pictures. The company was struggling financially and needed a hit so she was given her major début role in Alfred Hitchcock's British production, *Jamaica Inn*, in 1939. The audience cheered her after the première and besieged her for autographs. It was a box-office hit and Laughton then took her to Hollywood to play the female lead, as a spirited gypsy girl, Esmeralda, to his Quasimodo in RKO's *The Hunchback of Notre Dame*. RKO took over her contract from Mayflower and immediately put her into the remake of *A Bill of Divorcement* in 1940 and she was very much on her way.

The following year she really established herself, working with John Ford for the first time in his Oscar-winning *How Green Was My Valley*. She grew from those roles to go on and work for 20th Century Fox and develop a style which saw her cast as a stubborn, determined character on screen who could hold her own with a sword, a gun or her fists. In 1946 Maureen became a US citizen and three years later signed a contract with Universal where, for the first time, this multi-talented actress was allowed to sing and dance in *Baghdad*. She never did fulfil her ambition to take part in a full musical, although she would be allowed to sing in *The Quiet Man* where she and John Wayne would perform like Laurel and Hardy, in a field full of leprechauns.

The Cast

Barry Fitzgerald

Leprechaun-like is perhaps the best way to sum up Barry Fitzgerald. Born in Dublin on 10 March 1888 and christened William Joseph Shields, this impish, diminutive, whimsical and irascible character-actor was much loved wherever he went. Once asked where Fitzgerald left off and the part began, he said in that lovely brogue: 'I've long since forgotten. I suspect it's almost all me.' As the calculating village marriage-broker he would steal the show in *The Quiet Man*. Wiry and squint-faced, he was a notorious scene-stealer yet away from the stage or screen he was a gem of a man often said to have no vices whatsoever.

Although he was to gain international recognition for his characterisation of the small leprechaun-like Irishman, he became an actor almost by accident and did not not begin his stage career till the age of 40. It all started because of his love of hiking. One Sunday in 1914 while out walking, he struck up a casual acquaintance with another hiker who happened to be a member of the Abbey Theatre. He was invited to watch a performance from the wings and suddenly found himself pressed into service as an extra and pushed on to stage. That lit the spark of ambition and for the next 15 years he led the double life of civil servant by day and actor by night, adopting the name of a programme-seller at the theatre in an effort to keep his evening job a secret from his employers.

His first success was in *The Silver Tassie* in 1929. The following year he made his film début in Alfred Hitchcock's British production of Sean O'Casey's *Juno and the Paycock* in which he was the drunken, roistering Captain Boyle. In 1932 he toured the USA with the Abbey Players and thereafter appeared frequently on Broadway. It was his part as 'Fluther Good' in another Sean O'Casey play, *The Plough and the Stars*, which saw John Ford lure him to Hollywood where he was asked to play the same part in the film version. Apart from the occasional return to the stage, he remained in films for the rest of his life as the movie colony's Irishman-in-residence, playing those fanciful, heavily-accented, ethnic near-caricatures with much skill and charm. But his rise from junior civil servant to Hollywood stardom left him completely unaffected and this was a large part of his appeal. He inspired great affection among those who watched him on stage, screen or in real life. He was the gift of the Abbey Theatre to

Hollywood, very much the vogue in brogue, but despite his scene-stealing reputation he was a quiet, retiring person who, when in company, preferred to observe than be observed.

As the elderly, wise-cracking, none-too-saintly parish priest, Father Fitzgibbon, in Leo McCarey's *Going My Way* in 1944, he practically stole the show from Bing Crosby and won an Oscar for best supporting actor. Later he decapitated the gold statuette when practising golf shots in his living-room. Till this point Fitzgerald had never played anything but boozy old men on the American screen. He was as unlikely a priest as Crosby, but his delivery was always superb. Leo McCarey also won an Oscar as best director and one prominent Academy voter was heard to say: 'Anybody who can get two boozers like Crosby and Fitzgerald to act like convincing priests deserves all the honours you can give him.'

Mildred Natwick

Mildred Natwick landed the widow role after being introduced to John Ford by the great Henry Fonda. Born in 1908 in Baltimore, Maryland, her mother's family had arrived in America from England in the 1700s and her father's from Norway in the 1840s. Natwick is in fact a Norwegian name. She began her acting career in Washington DC in children's plays working for $5 a week. Fonda and another actor, Kent Smith, had invited her to join them in the late twenties and a decade later, on Fonda's recommendation and without having seen her act, Ford gave her the big breakthrough she sought in *The Long Voyage Home* in 1940. She was at her best in eccentric roles and in *Voyage* she played alongside John Wayne, Barry Fitzgerald, Ward Bond, Arthur Shields (Barry's brother) and Cyril McLaglen, brother of Victor.

Francis Ford

Still on a brotherly theme, Francis Ford, elder brother of John, was born in Portland, Maine in 1883, real name Francis O'Fearna. Like Victor McLaglen he was a restless type and he ran away from home at an early age and enlisted for the Spanish-American War. Having barely survived cholera, he was taken home by his father but ran away again and joined a circus, a forerunner for moving on to a stage career. With his new name he went into the silent-film industry which had moved from the east coast to the west and where he was to take the young John Ford, then Sean, under his wing when he arrived in Hollywood.

He was often portrayed as the grizzled, cheery westerner but by 1914 he had set up the Francis Ford Serial Company within the Universal City studios just outside Hollywood. On three large sets as many as 30 pictures could be in production simultaneously. He would land the part of the old, white-bearded man, Dan Tobin, in *The Quiet Man*, a name by which he was never referred to directly in the movie. The only reference is the voice of Sean Thornton's mother telling him how he used to be chased by Dan Tobin's bull. The name in Maurice Walsh's story is Matt Tobin.

Herbert J. Yates

Behind the cameras loomed the figure of Herbert J. Yates who was the autocratic owner of Republic Pictures. His word was law,

(Left to right) Francis Ford, John Wayne, Victor McLaglen and John Ford, with Barry Fitzgerald in front

55

especially when he insisted that his wife, Vera Hruba Ralston, a former East European ice-skating champion, should star in many of his productions. He even insisted on John Wayne acting alongside her, much to Wayne's annoyance.

Merian C. Cooper

Merian C. Cooper, Ford's Argosy partner, was as big a star as anyone on screen and lived out one of the most fascinating lives in the movie industry. Born in 1893 he was to achieve something Ford and Wayne had been denied – entry to the Annapolis Naval College, although he was expelled in his final year! Despite that he was to go on to great things and he was among the first American pilots sent to France in the First World War, and, just six weeks before the Armistice was declared, he was shot down over Mannheim in Germany and confined to a German hospital for some time. Despite having been severely wounded, he had saved his gunner's life by dragging him from the aircraft.

In 1919 he was offered a commission in the Polish Air Force and flew with great distinction in the Russian-Polish War, against the Bolshevics. He was again shot down, and imprisoned in Siberia but escaped and made his way back to the USA. After that he travelled the world making film-documentary classics in places like Persia and Siam. This launched him in the direction of Hollywood where he met John Ford in 1933. That same year Cooper made *King Kong* which was panned by the critics but became a huge box-office success. His friendship with Ford blossomed, no doubt because both had a great love of all things military. He would also strike up a friendship with Ward Bond and the three would enjoy each others company. In 1940 Cooper, again showing the spirit of an adventurer – a seeming prerequisite to be a member of the *Quiet Man* team – walked out on a huge salary of $100,000 a year and the vice-presidency of RKO to help organise the Flying Tigers, a mercenary band of pilots who flew for Chiang Kai-shek. The following year, while awaiting reassignment to the US Air Force, Pearl Harbour was attacked and he was quickly back in action and ended up Chief of Staff of Advanced Echelon for Air for General Douglas McArthur. He pioneered the first factory to manufacture parachutes – not surprising having been twice shot down in flames!

The Cast

Winton C. Hoch

When it came to shooting action Winton C. Hoch was regarded in Hollywood as the premier cinematographer and certainly one of the pioneers of the Technicolor process. There is no doubt that his special ability in capturing the beauty of Ireland in colour for the first time has been responsible for hundreds of thousands of tourists flocking to the country and Connemara in particular.

This former research physicist had a rather uneasy, sometimes turbulent, relationship with John Ford. In fact he reported the director to the American Society of Cinematographers during the filming of *She Wore a Yellow Ribbon* in 1949. He was shooting a desert scene when a storm brought some angry clouds across the sky. Hoch thought there was not enough light. Ford, using some expletives, ordered him to shoot. Hoch made his complaint then discovered that the scene looked so sensational on screen that it helped win him an Oscar! He was a creative artist and an optical scientist who in fact won three creative Oscars and a technical Academy Award. He would tinker on the set, adjusting dials, having everything perfectly lit, focused and framed. His sweeping Technicolor vistas were immense. He got his own back in *The Quiet Man* when Ford reckoned the light was poor and prepared for a delay. Hoch said 'I'm ready now, Jack.' The scene came back from the laboratory absolutely perfect! Ford would call him 'fussy' but between them they continued to produce classics.

Archie Stout

Archie Stout was Hoch's brilliant second-unit photographer. Born in 1886 he built a great reputation over many years in silent movies as well as sound in Hollywood. He began his career in 1914 and worked many times with John Ford, including on the 1937 Goldwyn-United Artists production of *The Hurricane*.

Like Hoch, he was one of Ford's wartime combat friends and in fact his son was killed while serving in one of Ford's units in France and was buried there. Archie Stout had been involved in many of John Wayne's early films and he worked on such classics as *Fort Apache*, *Wagonmaster* and *Rio Grande*. He would be 65 when shooting some of those magnificent *Quiet Man* scenes.

In the Footsteps of *The Quiet Man*

Victor Young

To match Hoch's vistas was the music of Victor Young, a great American composer born in 1900, who produced hundreds of movie scores and who collaborated with Ford to produce such wonderful music for *The Quiet Man*. He adapted the rollicking 'Fairy Reel', the rousing 'Wild Colonial Boy', the melodic 'Believe Me if All Those Endearing Young Charms' and the magnificent 'Isle of Innisfree'. Also included were 'The Young May Moon' by Thomas Moore, 'The Kerry Dances', 'Galway Bay' by Dr Andrew Colahan and Michael Donovan and 'The Humour is On Me Now', while the comical 'Mush, Mush, Mush, Tu-ral-i-adi' was joined by snatches from the 'Low-Backed Car', 'Gary Owen', 'The Rising of the Moon', 'I'll Take You Home Again Kathleen' and 'The Rakes of Mallow'.

Frank S. Nugent

Frank S. Nugent wrote the screenplay for *The Quiet Man* and was Ford's favourite collaborator. Born in 1908, he started out in his professional life as a journalist and became a highly respected and rather famous film critic with the *New York Times*. He was a ruddy-cheeked man with a typical American crew-cut and spectacles like milk-bottle bottoms, and had been taken to Hollywood by Darryl Zanuck in 1941. Half-Jewish and half-Irish, Ford often described him as 'my body and fender man' because he could always give a final high polish to scripts.

Nugent was impressed by Ford's musical choice for *The Quiet Man* and said at the time: 'He professes to have a tin ear for music, but he can carry a tune well for a man with no voice.' Ford taught Nugent to write out complete biographies of everyone in the film – including where they were born, educated, their politics and the like. Before a western, he would send Nugent to old Apache country to get the feel and smell of the land and he would give him novels and anything else relative to that period.

Nugent put the *Quiet Man* script together in just ten weeks after Welsh Novelist, Richard Llewellyn, who had written *How Green Was My Valley*, had, on Ford's instructions, expanded the Walsh story into a novella. Ford loved to work closely with his writers, although once the work was completed a writer would enter the studio at his peril. Nugent would work as he always did, a couple of hours in the morning and the same in the afternoon. But Ford would get him to stop for a few days at a time and just talk over what had been written. It was almost as if the director didn't want anything to break the leisurely pace of the story.

Contribution from the Abbey Theatre

Barry Fitzgerald was just one of many fine actors produced by Dublin's wonderful Abbey Theatre down through the years, a point not lost on John Ford who was astute enough to appreciate that they would lend their own brand of celtic magic to *The Quiet Man*.

It is one of the paradoxes of Irish history that, despite their flair for the dramatic and the fact they have produced quality actors for hundreds of years, the Irish nation has no tradition of theatre in the historic sense. Playwrights from Ludovic Barry in the early 17th century through to Samuel Beckett in the 20th have made distinguished contributions as have Wilde, Shaw, Sheridan, Goldsmith and Farquhar. And while Ireland has a literature in the Irish language stretching back to the early Christian period of 5000 AD, it was the decay of the Gaelic culture under British rule that created the anomaly. It took a memorable meeting between William Butler Yeats, well known as a poet of the Celtic Twilight, Edward Martyn, the wealthy Galway landowner and aspiring playwright, and Lady Gregory, herself a playwright, in Duras House, Kinvara, on the shores of Galway Bay in 1898 to create the dramatic movement which led to the Abbey Theatre taking shape. They wanted to give Ireland its own national theatre. Yeats was to say of Lady Gregory, 'She has been to me, mother, friend, sister and brother. I cannot realise the world without her – she brought to my wavering thoughts steadfast nobility.'

The Abbey Theatre, in Abbey Street, opened in 1904 and enjoyed great acclaim through the years, with tours to Broadway, 'By special arrangement with the Irish Free State Government', the posters claimed. But the theatre was gutted by fire in 1951. The playwright Sean O'Casey wrote at the time: 'It is only a temporary misfortune. We must build a better theatre. The old Abbey had a grand death anyway. A new Abbey for a new age; that's our job now.' The Queen's Theatre was leased until the Abbey was rebuilt on an adjacent site, which was completed in the mid-sixties after President de Valera had laid the foundation stone. It was decided to erect a plaque commemorating the Easter Rising of 1916 in the foyer which proclaims: 'It is a hard service they take that help me. Members of the Company and Staff of the Abbey Theatre who participated in the Rising of Easter Week 1916 – Sean Connolly, killed in action, Maire Nic Shiubhlaigh, Helena Molony, Ellen Bushell, Arthur Shields, Barney Murphy, Peadar Kearney, author of The Soldier's Song.'

Arthur Shields was a brother of Barry Fitzgerald and the man who would be cast by John Ford as the quiet, gentlemanly Reverend Cyril Playfair in *The Quiet Man*. Who would ever have thought that this mild-mannered soul was a man of courage who had fought against great odds in the cause of his country's freedom? Born in 1895, this Irish character actor spent many years in Hollywood with Barry after serving the Abbey well. Before making *The Quiet Man*, he had appeared in *The Plough and the Stars, Drums Along the Mohawk, The Long Voyage Home, The Keys of the Kingdom, The Corn is Green* and *The River*.

Another Abbey star, who like Barry Fitzgerald threatened to 'steal' *The Quiet Man*, was Jack McGowran, the pallid yes-man to Red Will Danaher. Born in Lower Beechwood Avenue, Ranelagh, Dublin he began his working life as an insurance salesman and part-time actor. He was a comical figure on and off screen and also found some time to indulge in some Shakespeare when he played Speed in *Two Gentlemen of Verona* at the Shakespeare Men's Theatre in Stratford-Upon-Avon. Born in 1916, his sharp features took him towards a career in the theatre and films and later television. *The Quiet Man* was his first movie and his first visit to Hollywood.

Others from the Abbey included Eileen Crowe, Mrs Elizabeth Playfair in the movie, who went on to Hollywood with McGowran to film interior shots. She joined the Abbey School of Acting in August 1921 and played the leading female role just six weeks later in Terence MacSwiney's play *The Revolutionist*. She later played Nora Helmar in *A Doll's House*, Mrs Borkman in *John Gabriel Borkman* and Jocasta in the Yeats version of *Oedipus*. She also appeared in most of the productions of George Bernard Shaw, W.B. Yeats, Lennox Robinson and Sean O'Casey. She visited almost every city in the United States and Canada during the

Jack McGowran

four Abbey tours there in the thirties, also playing with them in London, Paris and Florence.

May Craig, the lady seen in the opening railway-station sequences of *The Quiet Man*, was a link with the earliest Abbey days playing alongside Maire O'Neill and Sara Allgood in the original production of *The Playboy of the Western World* in 1907. She went on to act with great distinction in many Abbey productions including *Autumn Fire* by T. C. Murray and Shaw's *Arms and the Man*. Of her performance as the medium Mrs Henderson, in *The Words Upon the Window Pane*, Yeats said: 'When May Craig leaves the dressing-room she locks her door and leaves May Craig inside and becomes Mrs Henderson.'

Sean McClory, whose other films included *Beyond Glory, Rommell, Desert Fox* and *Les Misérables*, is cast as Glynn in *The Quiet Man*. He took part as the chubby-faced, pipe-smoking man alongside Charles FitzSimons, playing Forbes, the IRA commandant, and James Lilburn, who played Father Paul. Both FitzSimons and Lilburn are brothers of Maureen O'Hara. McClory was a former Abbey man but took part only in the Hollywood interior scenes. He was originally from Galway where his father had been a county councillor.

Other Abbey actors featured were Eric Gorman (the train guard) and Joseph O'Dea, brother of the better-known Abbey and Hollywood actor, Jimmy O'Dea, whose movies included *The Rising of the Moon* and *Derby O'Gill and the Little People*. Joseph played the train driver.

Chapter Four
CUT!

Herbert Yates had agreed a budget of $1.7 million for *The Quiet Man* but very quickly returned to his old ways, complaining about the script and the casting. Ford, who had worked with the top studios, was becoming more and more exasperated and John Wayne was growing unhappy in the knowledge he had got his friend and mentor involved with someone like Yates.

During pre-production in Hollywood, Yates threw another spanner in the works by summoning Wayne to his office and telling him the film would damage his career. He told Wayne he wanted nothing to do with it and would not be responsible for the consequences. He insisted it was the wrong type of movie for Wayne, even though he knew the part had been specially written with the actor in mind. Yates, who had made part of his fortune from the button industry, tobacco trade and some shrewd dealing on Wall Street, seemed to be hell-bent on sabotaging everything. With each passing day his paranoia grew and he convinced himself that Ford had sold him what he constantly referred to as 'a phoney art-house movie'. The drama heightened considerably when Yates, who had sweated over an injection of $1.5 million into *Rio Grande*, became apoplectic about his latest outlay and went back on his word to Ford. He demanded the budget be trimmed but the director had already cut it to near enough the bone. This prompted the following telegram from Ford to Wayne, who was having his first holiday in years: 'After much fuss and feathers, much wrangling, fist-fights and harsh words the budget is set excepting, of course, for your salary which you will have to take up when you get back. I'm a nervous wreck.'

But his cherished film was still in danger and Ford turned to his friend Wayne who, after years of battling with Yates, had succeeded in getting a percentage of Republic box-office profits, and asked him to settle for a flat fee. Maureen O'Hara recalled: 'John Ford asked John Wayne and me to take a cut and because we had all waited so long and so badly wanted to make the movie we agreed. John Wayne accepted $100,000 and I got $65,000. I even took down the script in shorthand and typed it as it meant so much to me.'

Maureen O'Hara's contract for the part of Mary Danaher was for ten weeks and contained the following remarks: 'Co-star preceded only by Wayne in type of same size and prominence used for Wayne. If name of any member of cast displayed above title, her name to appear above title. If her name displayed below title, lines upon which her name and Wayne's name appear to be immediately preceded by "starring". No obligation to give credit in ads four column inches or less.' The contract is dated 22 May 1951. Other contracts of the same date are:

> Barry Fitzgerald, for the part of Michaeleen Oge Flynn, the marriage-broker, with a salary of $7,500 a week, guaranteed for eight weeks, starting on/or about 7 June 1951, with a 'co-star billing screen and paid ad.';
>
> Ward Bond, for the part of Lonergan, the priest, with a salary of $5,000 a week, guaranteed for four weeks 'plus 3 weeks free if needed', starting on/about his '1st appearance before the camera in Ireland' with his 'Billing to be left to the discretion of Mr. John Ford and in the event of Mr. Ford's unavailability, or if the billing has not been set up at the time the main title is prepared, billing will be at the discretion of Mr. Herbert J. Yates or his successor';
>
> Victor McLaglen, for the part of Will Danaher, with a salary of $25,000 for the picture ('$5,000/5 plus whatever free weeks are required to complete the role'), again beginning at his first appearance before the camera and with a similar billing status as Ward Bond;
>
> Arthur Shields, for the part of the Reverend Playfair with a salary of $1,250 a week for six weeks, again beginning from

his first appearance in front of the camera but 'in any event not later than on/or about June 9, 1951', and with a 'feature billing on screen';

Mildred Natwick, for the part of Mrs Tillane, the widow Will Danaher is chasing, with a salary of $1,000 a week for eight weeks, under the same conditions as Arthur Shields;

and Francis Ford, John's brother, for the part of the old man, Tobin, with a salary of $500 for one week's filming, starting on 6 July 1951.

Obviously, after all the chicanery by Yates, there was tension in the air as the time approached for the cast and crew to leave Hollywood for Ireland. It wasn't helped by the fact that Wayne's second wife, a Mexican named Chata, accompanied him. So did the four children from his first marriage, Michael, 17, Toni, 15, Patrick, 14, and Melinda, 12, who were given roles as extras. Since his divorce from first wife, Josephine, Wayne had tried to spend as many weekends as possible with the children but being away on location so much made that difficult and they were allowed by their mother to spend the summer months with Wayne. When they heard he was going back to the land of their forefathers they all clamoured to go and Wayne agreed. His marriage to Chata was already on the rocks, mainly due to her drinking sprees. These proved irritating to John Ford. Twelve months later there would be divorce proceedings when Chata would demand $9,000 a month plus the house, the cars, the savings and investments, virtually a repeat of what Wayne was reputed to have given to Josephine seven years earlier. It was a state of affairs which would rumble on and even a year earlier, as filming started, Wayne must have known the torture which lay ahead in his personal life.

However, the summer of 1951 saw Ireland at its best with good dry weather and a fair amount of sunshine. And, despite daily phone calls and cables from Yates, which just about burned up postmistress Mary Gibbons's village switchboard in Cong, and the presence of Chata, the cast, housed in nearby Ashford Castle, enjoyed the weather, the scenery and the warmth of the local community, not to mention their pubs. Ashford Castle, today one of the great hotels of the world, was not quite as luxurious in those days, with little heat and no elevators which did not please the Yanks. But Wayne loved the company of Ford,

Ashford Castle on Lough Corrib

McLaglen and Bond, who, like him, had been founder members of The Young Men's Purity, Total Abstinence and Yachting Association. This unlikely-sounding body had been founded along with various other actors and writers, and at weekends they would live on Ford's yacht, the *Araner*, and during the week they would congregate at the Hollywood Athletic Club. The object of their hell-raising activities, they said, was the cause of alcoholism, with a bit of boating, fishing and anything else they fancied thrown in. The not-so-hilarious side of their habits were to come later when half the group suffered health problems. Ford became an alcoholic while Bond was to die young of a heart attack brought on by high blood pressure. Wayne, it appeared, could swig tequila without any damage except to his crumbling marriages.

Meanwhile, back to that glorious summer in Cong, the primary location and a historic area where medieval kings and chieftains, seeking an escape from their warring, turbulent lives, refreshed and recharged themselves among the cloisters of the abbey. Cong had faded before the onslaughts of pagan invaders and reforming conquerors; now John Ford was about to put it back on the map. The village had taken its name from the Gaelic 'cunga' which means 'isthmus' and it is built on a three-mile-wide natural bridge of limestone underneath which the waters of Lough Corrib and Lough Mask meet. Ford was by this time well aware that a great deal would hang on *The Quiet Man* in terms of its success or failure. It would go a long way to determine his future and his attitude to film-making. Even after arriving in Ireland he began to harbour doubts, after all the years of chasing his cherished dream, if he in fact had a picture on his hands. This was probably down to all the hassle he was receiving from Yates. The one consolation was that the Republic boss had remained in Hollywood although he would scrutinise production reports flown daily from Shannon Airport along with reels of film sent back for processing.

One telegram which was sent from his daughter, Barbara, who was assisting editor Jack Murray 'cut' the film back in Hollywood, must have lifted some of the clouds around Ford. Dated 20 June 1951 it read: 'The film is beautiful. We have received five days' work and it looks just like a fairyland. They really hit it on the head when they named it the Emerald Isle. I never believed any place could be so lovely.' But telegrams from Yates constantly threatened to shut down the movie if Ford went 'one cent' over budget. The other instruction was that the movie must not run 'a single second' over 120 minutes. Yates was also making moves, behind Ford's back, to change the title of what he called 'an egg-head movie' to *The Man Untamed* or *Uncharted Voyage*. There would be other such clumsy attempts in the future. And in addition to the Yates factor, the film, which had been carefully planned and prepared, was proving difficult to make because the magnificent scenery and Irish pace of life were distracting the crew. And there was a further problem with locals hanging out of their windows and wandering into shots.

All of this was making Ford unhappy. He was further handi-capped by pain in his left hand caused by injuries sustained in his hectic role in the war, during which he was honoured in the crucial Battle of Midway against the Japanese. At one stage in Cong the pain was so bad that it put him out of action for a day. However, the show went on, with John Wayne, Lee Lukather and Andrew McLaglen, son of Victor, who was an assistant director, taking the second unit to shoot part of the horse-race scene in North Connemara. While he was never quite in danger of requiring the Last Rites, Ford, who had a great suspicion of most clerics, had taken his own priest to Ireland and put him down on Herbert Yates's bill as a technical adviser! When the pain disappeared he relaxed with a soft drink and had the cast in tears of laughter with accounts of how he had talked Yates into parting with *The Quiet Man* budget.

'I took him to the most picturesque part of Connemara and showed him a little white-washed cottage with shutters and a thatched roof. "There it is," I told him, with tears running down my cheeks, "the house where I was born."'

'And was it?' inquired one of his captivated audience.

'Of course not,' said Ford. 'I was born in the States.' Then resuming his exaggerated tale he said: 'Yates started crying too and said: "You can do *The Quiet Man* for a million and a half."' Of course Yates hadn't set foot in Connemara and this was Ford using some kind of escape-valve and having a tilt at his adversary.

Chapter Five
FILMING IN THE EMERALD ISLE

As the *Quiet Man* team arrived in Ireland in 1951 there was an electricity supply crisis, the potato crop was in danger from blight and there was the threat of a strike by cinema staff throughout the country. The village of Cong and its surrounding area were in fact still awaiting the arrival of the electric light but in other parts of Ireland the Electricity Supply Board was furiously advertising in all of the newspapers, warning people that rationing was in force and if they exceeded their agreed power allowance the supply would be cut. They banned the use of electric fires and arranged for 40,000 tons of turf to be transported from the bogs in the south-west to help fire the power stations.

The Irish Times of 5 June informed its readers that a film crew had arrived in Co. Mayo: 'An official of Republic Pictures has announced that, as a result of "The Quiet Man" being filmed here, there will be a gain to Ireland of $600,000 (£215,000). One hundred local people will be used as extras as in the case of the British production of "Henry V" in Co. Wicklow a few years ago. A small committee is to meet in Dublin to determine the salaries for people with parts to play in the film.' The author of the short article also came up with a very good forecast when he said, before a camera had rolled, that the movie would win John Ford an Oscar!

On 6 June the same publication reported: 'Maureen O'Hara, John Wayne and Victor McLaglen arrived yesterday at Shannon Airport and Miss O'Hara was met by her parents Mr and Mrs FitzSimons. Miss O'Hara said the script was really a great one and there is no attempt at stage Irishism. "For that reason I am glad to have been asked to play in it," she said. John Wayne flew in from Caracas, Venezuela, where he had been enjoying his first vacation in five years. He referred to John Ford as "Bo" Feeney, his real name. He made his first film with Ford in 1928 when he was a student. Victor McLaglen passed through Dublin on his way to Shannon with Barry Fitzgerald and Arthur Shields. The film will be in Technicolor.'

That same edition reported that a country-wide cinema strike had just been averted after it had been agreed to pay adult males over 23 a 12-shilling-a-week rise, females and adults between 18 and 23 a rise of seven shillings a week with four shillings a week extra for junior staff. A further report noted that a new season at the old Abbey Theatre in Dublin would feature Eric Gorman and May Craig in Sean O'Casey's *The Plough and the Stars*.

The local Galway paper, the *Connacht Tribune*, was also monitoring events and on 16 June it reported that Ward Bond had been the last of the *Quiet Man* team to arrive at Shannon Airport as he had been filming in Hollywood. It was also reported that John Murphy was having to turn weary travellers away from his door. When they saw the Pat Cohan sign above his shop they thought they could buy a drink not realising it was an ordinary shop and the sign a film prop!

Maureen O'Hara told a *Tribune* reporter: 'I've never experienced such luck on any film. When we require brilliant sunshine we get it. As far as I'm concerned Ireland is the star of the picture. No one has ever put Ireland on the screen in Technicolor before. This is something I've wanted to do, it's been on the go since the mid-forties.' Miss O'Hara then told the story of how, being so keen to get the movie off the ground, she took down the script in shorthand and typed it up, skills learned at 'Miss Galway's School for Young Ladies' in her native Dublin where she lived near the Dropping Well at No. 13 Churchtown Road on the south side of the city. Miss Galway's was a place she would go late in the afternoon or evenings to brush up those additional skills. 'My mother, knowing all of us were involved, or going to be involved, with the theatre, would worry about what could happen at an audition and she wanted us to have an alternative career so if we were turned down we could walk out knowing we could earn a living doing something else.'

Pat Cohan's bar, still the same today as it was in 1951

Another report revealed: 'Maureen O'Hara referred to the Joyce's cottage [used as White O' Mornin'] at Tirnikill, Maam, as "Just what we wanted. It is a beautiful little cottage with a stream in front and with stepping stones across. One would think some set designer just dreamed it as it is."'

One of the men who discovered the cottage and the other locations was Lord Killanin who recalled: 'It was a good find because of its stream and the fact it was thatched and absolutely unspoiled. Originally, Republic Pictures asked me what they should pay Mr Joyce, the owner, and I said about £25 a week. But that part of the budget must have been healthy because they paid him £100 a day!'

The *Connacht Tribune* reported: 'Yesterday tradesmen were at work in the cottage putting in larger windows and a new coat of thatch. A new half-door was also installed.' By coincidence, *The Irish Times* carried an article around the same time on how an American judge had come back to his native land and had been astounded that people had removed the half-doors from their cottages and replaced them with modern one-piece doors.

As work progressed on the cottage, the *Tribune* of 23 June reported:

> There is a temporary Hollywood in the west of Ireland, with a wholesome friendly atmosphere. Victor McLaglen wakened out of a snooze on a deckchair to offer a warm handshake. John Wayne was like an old friend you had known for years and told you with a laugh the story of tourists pulling up at the Cohan sign looking for food and drink. Maureen O'Hara hopped down from a sidecar in which she had been on her first date with the returned Yank and spoke of the film as if it was something happening to her in real life. She wore a summer frock and tweed jacket, the very antithesis of a temperamental, neurotic star. She spoke about her relations in Castlebar and her seven-year-old daughter, Bronwyn, who was with her and had just made her first communion. She also spoke of her stand-in, Etta Vaughan, who had been spotted for the part by Wingate Smith, brother-in-law to John Ford.
>
> Barry Fitzgerald toddled around the set in bowler hat and, with a whimsical smile, his two hands containing his pipe and tobacco pouch. Andy McLaglen, who received no help

John Wayne was a big man but, at six-foot eight, Andrew McLaglen was even bigger!

from his father, Victor, in getting into the film business, was second assistant-director to Wingate Smith and six-foot seven and three-quarters tall. He wanted to join the US Air Force but was turned down because they had a six-foot limit! Arthur Shields, brother of Barry Fitzgerald, was an old IRA man who took a prominent part in the fight for Irish independence. Francis and Eamonn Feeney, brothers of John Ford, are also here. Ford was deeply moved when he visited the family home in Tourbeg, Spiddal, and saw the room and very bed in which his grandfather had been born.

The weekly Connacht paper reported on 30 June: 'John Wayne and Maureen O'Hara rode down Cong main street at break-neck speed on a tandem with Miss O'Hara precariously on the back. They did this several times, cutting the angular corner outside Cohan's with inches to spare. A doctor was on standby in case of injury to the stars.' The same edition carried a short article stating that entry to Ashford Castle was 2/6d but the money would be returned if a visitor bought lunch, high tea or dinner.

As filming progressed the coming of electricity presented John Ford and his technicians with an unusual headache. Because of the rocky terrain on the outskirts of Cong, the ESB had to use gelignite to blast holes for the erection of the electricity poles. The blasts were being picked up on the soundtrack of the movie and there had to be a quick pow-wow between the ESB and Ford. The company agreed to postpone placing some poles in the village itself as Cong was supposed to represent the Ireland of 1920. The *Connacht Tribune* reported that, while electricity production was down 25 per cent from the previous year, the Cong rural electrification scheme had been switched on at 11 p.m. on Friday 6 July.

At a function held in Ashford Castle to celebrate the switch on of the electric current, Very Reverend M. Canon Carney, parish priest, Cong, expressed the hope that the Erne Scheme would become the symbol of unity between North and South.

He hoped it would replace the old symbol of separation because rural electrification was a blessing not merely to the Ireland of today but to the Ireland of the future. Reverend Father Lyons, chairman of the Cong Rural Electrification Committee, paid tribute to his committee and went on to say that at one time it appeared that, because of the reluctance of many in the area to accept the current, the E.S.B. would have to by-pass Cong for a considerable time. Mr McCarthy, superintendent, E.S.B., Galway, said that people had begun to realise that electricity was the most economic fuel of all. Among a company of no fewer than seven clergy were guests Lord Killanin, John Ford, John Wayne and Barry Fitzgerald who were treated to some Irish songs by the Reverend Malachy Eaton of Claremorris.

The *Tribune*, under a headline of 'A SNEEZE MIGHT COST $200', went on to say:

Visitors while production work is in progress are definitely out and director John Ford frowns on any attempt to interfere with his team once they have clocked in and understandably so, for the amount of organisation, precision and coordination of the work of actors, directors, managers, electricians, extras and others that is concentrated on one short take has to be seen to be realised. Mr Lukather, the production manager, on the other hand, has to keep in mind, with the cost of production running into a number of thousands of pounds a day, an untimely sneeze after 'quiet please' is more likely to cost Republic Pictures a few hundred dollars.

Nothing could be further from the truth than that the film stars look different in real life. Barry Fitzgerald was unmistakable as he sat in a side-car waiting for his cue. With knees crossed, an old bowler hat and the familiar pipe gripped in the side of his mouth, Barry sat for hours placidly studying his script. Later, sitting on the grass during his lunch break, he inquired about some of his old colleagues at the Abbey Theatre and recalled that Liam Redmond, who worked in Cong some years ago on the film 'Captain Boycott', played alongside him in New York in 'The White Steed'. The dark glasses, false beards and camouflage of the sort we had been led to believe film stars carry around to avoid autograph hunters, have been left behind in Hollywood.

Missing also from this galaxy of stars and celebrities is the tinder-box temperament and the reserve that are supposed to be characteristic of Hollywood deities, and John Wayne,

Barry Fitzgerald, Victor McLaglen, Ward Bond and the rest have been voted unanimously, by the hundreds who have come daily to see their favourites in person, a bunch of 'regular fellers'. All those who have been fortunate enough to meet the stars outwith their working hours have been delighted to find them not only very willing to oblige by signing autographs and posing for photographs but anxious to spend a while chatting about fishing, their past films or anything under the sun.

Further reports announced:

On Sunday evening Ward Bond brought a five-pound trout off the lake and right proud he was, as it was the best catch of the day. It was also the first brown trout he had ever caught and on that account it was suggested he have it mounted. On hearing that they come up to 17 pounds on the Corrib, Ward said: 'Aw heck, I'll catch one of the bigger ones later,' and he decided to have the five-pounder for breakfast.

Victor McLaglen, after admiring the beauty of the Cong Woods and drinking in mighty lung-fulls of the country air as he stood on the steps of Ashford Castle, said: 'My wish for you is that your people be as happy as your countryside is pretty.' Victor, although born in England, can lay some claims to our nationality by virtue of the many occasions in which he has appeared on film as an Irishman.

Mr John Ford is anxious to recruit more local labour. Already some carpenters and painters have been commissioned. Sign boards and traders names that appear above shop doors will be changed temporarily. Wagon-loads of equipment and busloads of special workers, plus stunt men have arrived in Cong. Brian O'Higgins and other Abbey Players have been offered minor roles.

The Americans are non-plussed by the length of our midsummer day, daylight finishing in California about eight-thirty or 9p.m. When told that 'summertime' was brought into force in order to save daylight, they asked the obvious question: 'Why not get up earlier in the morning and save the daylight then?' And they received the obvious answer: 'We have to save it at night because we don't get up earlier!'

Lord Killanin recalled:

> Winnie Hoch, the cinematographer, constantly had problems
> with the light and often thought his meter was wrong because
> the light was so bright. But, of course, the light in Galway
> is very bright because of the reflections from the Atlantic.
> Winnie would always have his back to the actors, checking
> his light and his angles and an infuriated Jack Ford would rasp:
> 'Never employ a cameraman to direct a film because he never
> sees what's going on.'

Under the headline 'JUDY SHAUGHNESSY WAS TOAST
OF THE FILM STARS', the *Tribune* reported:

> When John Ford held a Press reception at Ashford Castle
> Hotel on Monday the star of the occasion was not one of
> his screen celebrities but Miss Shaughnessy of Houndswood
> Cross, Cong. It was the eve of her wedding and she was
> spending her last day on duty as a waitress. The following
> morning she became Mrs Michael Coen of Cross, and, at
> the informal dinner at which Press representatives met

*Main village street in Cong (opposite Cohan's) 1951: it is Wayne's car parked
outside of Clarke's*

Mr Ford and the members of his cast, Mr Ford proposed a toast to Judy and a presentation was made to her on behalf of the cast by Maureen O'Hara.

This public-spirited attitude continued when it was reported that, 'all the cast of the film "The Quiet Man" will attend the Society for the Prevention of Cruelty to Children garden fête in the grounds of Spiddal House on Sunday afternoon next. Patrons may meet them and be photographed with them. A polaroid camera will be available.'

Another *Tribune* article under the headline 'HOLLYWOOD TAKES OVER VILLAGE OF CONG' reported:

A dance organised by the English section of the film unit was held on Friday night. John Ford, Maureen O'Hara and practically all members of the unit attended and it proved a very enjoyable function. What with cigars, chewing gum, dollar bills, American accents and brilliant sunshine, Cong has taken on a Californian look.

When you put your nose outside the door you have an equal chance of bumping into a film star, a director, a property master, a stunt man or an ordinary native Irishman. 'Native' is the adjective that defines the main difference between the local people and the visitors, for the latter are to a great extent Irish-American. Director Ford's association with the people of Spiddal is already well-known, still a Connacht Tribune representative was surprised to hear a Hollywood Oscar winner, in his American accent, tell him he was still 'cineal bodhar' (deafened) from the drone of the plane engines on his journey to Ireland, and that he was a 'col cuigear' (cousin) of Michael Droighnea, a teacher from Furbough. Those who would like to have a long chat with Mr Ford would be well advised to forget all about Hollywood and film stars and be prepared to discuss the people of Connemara, the Cong struggle towards Irish independence, the Irish language and his Irish relations. He is very proud of his Irish parentage and mentioned he was the 11th child in his family.

On his first visit to Ireland is Tom Carmen, sound supervisor for the unit. He is so keen a fisherman that he is causing his pals concern by neglecting his meals to be out with a rod.

Filming in the Emerald Isle

Though I assured him that fly-fishing was an absolute loss this season he is so orthodox a fisherman that he would not use a worm in any circumstances. Tom's grandmother came from Ballyhaunis. She often called him a 'spailpin' (tinker) and a 'bladairin' (blether). When he learned the exact meaning of the words he said his grandmother could not have chosen better words to describe him in his scampish youth.

Art director Frank Hotaling [like Carmen mentioned in the movies opening titles], is likely to be mistaken for a leading man. Tall, dark and handsome, he hides behind shaded glasses and speaks with a deep voice which, if set to music, should cause Frank Sinatra fans to swoon. His name does not suggest Irish connections. 'I can't say I'm Irish,' said Frank, 'but my mother's name was Corcoran.'

Busiest man of all is property master 'Ace' Holmes. Having acquired a rocking-cradle that was stowed away in an attic for the past 30 years (the baby is now 6′ 2″) his chief headache now is to procure an old-time four-poster wooden bed. Those anxious to part with their old four-poster should not dispatch the article until it has first been examined by Mr Holmes, for the one needed is of very specific requirements. The one regret of 'Ace' who has successfully found a set of pewter mugs, a couple of barrels and miscellaneous other things, is that he has had to come to Ireland just when the golf competition of Republic Pictures Golf Club was about to start. He is one of the leading lights of the club and has decided to put in extra time on the Ashford links.

Under the headline 'FILM "BAR" WAS BUT A MIRAGE' appeared:

In flagrant defiance of the licensing laws, Pat Cohan's bar, Cong, was an open house on Sunday and thirsty travellers hastened to avail themselves of this unexpected opportunity of having a 'quick one'. Pat Cohan, the proprietor, will not appear at the next assises, however, to answer to the State for this deliberate breach of the law; for neither Pat nor his bar really exist outside of the story of the film 'The Quiet Man'. Mr John Murphy, merchant, the front of whose premises have been changed to look like a bar for filming purposes, has had a busy time all week explaining the position to would-be 'froth-blowers'.

Another report in the *Tribune* stated:

> Names like Robert Rideout, Albert Harrison, Arthur Greene, Dick Merrick, Tommy O'Sullivan, Jim Fletcher and Jonathan MacDonald will not appear on the screen in the introductory titles of 'The Quiet Man', yet each and every one of those lads is a vital part of the machine that is engaged in putting on to celluloid the Technicolor capers of Barry Fitzgerald and the rest. They are members of the crew of technicians who have been sent from London by their firm, Mole-Richardson, to take care of the lighting and equipment and has branches in Britain, USA, India and all over the world. Wherever a film is being made those boys are almost sure to be there. They have lately been in Canada and previously to Germany and Italy. But mostly their work is done in England. Almost all their engagements are for newsreels, documentaries and television and they have beamed their lights in Buckingham Palace and No 10 Downing Street.

The report added that Sergeant P. Moran, a native of Knocknageesha, Kilmaine, had been 'temporarily appointed to Cong' as had Sergeant P. Gallagher, a native of Glenties, Donegal, because of the crowds the filming was attracting to the area.

The *Tribune*'s 7 July issue stated that: 'Fourteen bus-loads of tourists pulled into Cong on Thursday evening,' and that some local men had been employed as stand-ins for the stars. 'Mr Jim Morrin is doubling for Barry Fitzgerald, Paddy Clarke for Ward Bond, Joe Mellotte of Neale for John Wayne and Stephen Lydon for Victor McLaglen.'

Under the headline 'FILM EXTRAS HAD RINGSIDE SEATS' appeared:

> A call for 120 extras to take part in 'The Quiet Man' in the farmyard at Ashford at the weekend got a very enthusiastic response, especially as it was learned that the main event to be filmed was the showdown between Sean, the returned Yank of the story [John Wayne], and the villainous gambeen man

[Victor McLaglen] who tried the Yank's patience just once too often. The extras were the crowd that formed the ring for the battle of the giants and, with hundreds of others who came to look on, they had a thoroughly enjoyable day watching those two stalwarts fight a dogged 'fight' from one end of the hay field to the other.

Action was the order of the day and Maureen O'Hara did not escape a large share of the knocks, having spent most of one day being dragged and pushed about by an angered 'husband'.

Two local men, Jim McVeigh, Dringeen, and Robert Foy, Cong [see the following chapter], had the lights and cameras all to themselves when they played a short scene with a speaking part in Maam Valley. The unit travelled to Ballyglunin on Monday to take some shots of the railway station there situated between Athenry and Tuam. The train, hired from CIE for the occasion, had carriages of the 1920s type. Three railwaymen were taken in the 'shots'. They were John Monaghan, Galway Road, Tuam, driver of the train; Gabriel Barrett, fireman; Joe Mullen, guard and T. Niland, station master [again, see the next chapter].

That report on the railway staff driving the train is of particular interest to me in that it is yet another *Quiet Man* coincidence. While looking for Ballyglunin Station (Castletown) I took a wrong turning after leaving Tuam and several miles along a deserted country road realised I was heading in the wrong direction. Suddenly, out of the torrential rain and mist emerged a figure, pulling a hood tightly around his head and face against the elements. I asked for directions and he told me I would have to go back to Tuam. I offered the fellow a lift and during the few minutes he was in the car he asked me why I was going to Ballyglunin. I told him about the researching of this book and he said he had known the driver of the train. 'We called him "Farmer John Monaghan" because after working with CIE he took over some land and he delivered milk in Tuam. I remember when I was a youngster he told me he had driven the train in *The Quiet Man*. He died a year or so ago and I think his wife moved to England.' This lad had been born long after the making of the movie yet he was able to impart information which was verified

Ward Bond (left) gets some advice from a local clergyman

by checking the old newspaper files in Galway and at the National Library, Dublin.

Another newspaper report of the time informed its readers that Ward Bond had featured in a scene at Ashford Bridge. 'Despite the water in the Cong River being so cold on its way from Lough Mask, he kept smiling through his ducking.'

Lord Killanin recalled an amusing tale from that day. He said: 'Ward was playing the priest and leaning on a wall beside the bridge to Ashford Castle. A well-dressed lady approached him and said: "Mr Bond can I have a word with you?" Ward courteously said: "Yes ma'am." She added: "You are playing a Catholic priest and you have your hand in your pocket. No Catholic priest ever puts his hand in his pocket."

'John Ford, who had overheard this exchange, immediately interjected saying: "Ma'am, you're absolutely right, only in other people's."'

Another of Lord Killanin's anecdotes recalled part of the famous horse-race scene being shot. 'It was done at Tully Strand in North Connemara. Duke Wayne's black horse was actually my own hunter and a very quiet animal. Despite that he couldn't ride it and said: "What an f ★★★ awful horse you've given me." I suddenly realised Duke had never ridden on a hunting saddle before and, if you watch the film very carefully, you will see that his stand-in is on a hunting saddle and Duke on a cowboy saddle which had to be specially and quickly flown over from the States.'

As filming progressed the *Connacht Tribune* reported:

On the set between the showers on Monday last were Barry Fitzgerald, Arthur Shields, Victor McLaglen, Mildred Natwick and English stage actor, Philip Stainton [he played the visiting Anglican bishop], and John Wayne. Mr Wayne had a quiet day but assisted the technicians. Ward Bond, after a morning in fruitless search of a trout from the Corrib, appeared in priestly garb but found that no work awaited him. Maureen O'Hara was also put out of business by the rain. All these plus Eileen Crowe, May Craig, Joe O'Dea, Eric Gorman, Francis Ford, Jack McGowran, Charlie and Jim FitzSimons (the latter having the stage name James Lilburn) attended an informal dinner afterwards. Director John Ford says if anyone is the producer of this film it is Very Reverend

M. Canon Carney, parish priest, Cong, with, as assistant producer, Reverend L. Lyons. He was deeply indebted to both these priests, he said. [One wonders if he repeated the story of Ward Bond having his hand in his pocket!] A 1923 Morris Cowley, the property of Mr O'Sullivan, Cornamon, is the newest star to appear in the film. Up to the time Arthur Shields took the wheel it had always been owner-driven since Mr O'Sullivan bought it new.

Eight hundred pounds approximately has been paid in wages to extras alone in the past six days in Cong.

Chapter Six
THE EXTRAS CAST

MARY GIBBONS, Cong postmistress since 4 October 1943
ROBERT FOY, Cong villager
MICHAEL AND BRIDIE HOPKINS, from Dringeen, near Cong
ETTA VAUGHAN, stand-in for Maureen O'Hara
MARY FARRAGHER, occupier of the 'Danaher' house.
JACK MURPHY, owner of 'Pat Cohan's Bar'
MARGARET NILAND, occupier of the 'Castletown' railway house
JOE MELLOTTE, stand-in for John Wayne
JIM FAHY, retired Cong schoolteacher and author of *The Glories of Cong*
FRED O'CONNOR, owner of the 'Emily O'Connor' shop in the cattle-fair scene

The chosen have become few, in and around Cong, but those invited to take part as stand-ins and extras way back in the summer of 1951 still hold the most cherished memories of perhaps the most exciting time of their lives.

Mary Gibbons, who is still postmistress, recalls:

> We had heard rumours for some time about a film being made and, despite being postmistress, I think I was probably the last to hear about it! My first reaction was to speak to Mr Noel Huggart the then owner of Ashford Castle because there was only one telephone line to serve the village. He was the man who had put Cong on the map after taking over the castle from the Guinness family and he confirmed the Americans

were coming. I told him we would have to do something about the telephone situation but he put the onus very much on me although he said to use his name in any way which might be helpful. I did and lo and behold we got a second line in next to no time.

Robert Foy, a lad in his 20s during filming, recalls:

At a time when the working man's average wage was around £3 10/- a week I was offered nine pounds by Republic Pictures. I was doing a little farming work at the time so this kind of added money was terrific.

Several of the scenes remain vivid in my mind despite the passing of the years. I remember, for instance, that the very first of the major scenes involving the stars was of Maureen O'Hara with the flock of sheep as she is spotted for the first time by John Wayne on his journey from the railway station with Barry Fitzgerald. It was filmed in the grounds of Ashford Castle with a local shepherd and his dog just wide of the camera-shots to make sure everything went smoothly. That spot is now the third fairway of the Ashford Castle golf course. None of us who were there that day will ever forget the way Miss O'Hara just walked into that shot and into the movie.

That memory was superbly described by the excellent cinema reviewer, Lindsay Anderson, who wrote:

Sean's first glimpse of Mary Kate is presented with a pre-Raphaelite relish for sharp and varied colouring, as well as a kindred romanticism of view; a fairy-tale shepherd girl, auburn-haired, scarlet skirted, dressed in two shades of blue, driving her sheep down the rocky dell, yellow gorse in the foreground, the countryside opening out greener in the distance. Then her backward glancing at Sean, as she moves slowly out of frame. Such close-ups in *The Quiet Man*, and this was the most memorable, have an intense communication of mood which take the breath away and give the film's language a sustained dignity of direct statement.

The first scene shot in the grounds of Ashford Castle as Maureen O'Hara makes her entrance

Bridie Hopkins:

> I was about 30 at the time, just married, and I remember my
> parents, with whom my husband and I stayed, and neighbours
> chiding me and my friends for working with the film company
> on a Sunday. Six of us, all Catholics, had to go into the
> Protestant Church and walk out in front of Maureen O'Hara
> as John Wayne offered her the holy water out of the font.
> Our parents were very unhappy about us going into another
> church and it was actually suggested that we mention it in our
> next confessions. Mind you, those were different times and we
> were all very innocent and shy.

Among Lord Killanin's many anecdotes is one of the holy water
scene:

> We used the interior of the Catholic Church in Cong, with its
> magnificent Harry Clarke stained-glass window, preserved to

this day in the reconstructed church, and the exterior of the Church of Ireland just a few hundred yards away at the exit gates from Ashford Castle. Jack Ford was keen to capture Clarke's work in the movie — even though he had to slow down the camera, which made Duke Wayne's walk a little stranger than usual as he came down the aisle. [Clarke, a Dublin artist born a hundred years ago of an English father and Irish mother, is now recognised internationally as a bizarre genius of his age.]

Using the Protestant Church led to trouble for Jack and I. The holy water font was taken from outside the Catholic Church and placed at the door of the Church of Ireland for the patty-fingers scene. Well, it was left there by mistake and the following Sunday when the Protestants turned up they objected strongly to the minister, who had given permission for filming, over what they reckoned to be a Papish intrusion. Jack and I were then asked to go and see the minister who had been paid for the use of his facilities but had now been reported to his bishop by an angry flock. So we went to see if we could placate the bishop who happened to be my father-in-law's bishop and who didn't like us in any case. He never even asked us to sit down and Jack was hopping mad. The bishop wanted us to delete the scene so we explained that it cost about £10,000 a day and this was four or five days' work. Needless to say, we kept the scene very much in. On reflection it's quite comical when you think about the precarious situation of the minister in the film, Mr Playfair, trying to impress his bishop that the parish should stay open, and the fact he has to depend on the Catholics 'cheering like Protestants' to help save his job.

Bridie Hopkins continued:

The stars were all so nice and would pose with us for photographs. We would run about wearing Connemara shawls and cheer John Wayne and Maureen O'Hara as Barry Fitzgerald drove the horse and trap. We were involved in a lot of the scenes although it seemed they only used a fraction of the film they actually shot. Barry Fitzgerald was the star of the show. He was terrific and we all loved him. He was exactly the same off screen as he was on it. There's no doubt the film brought a lot of much-needed money to the area and, with my husband and I both getting 30 bob a day, it was some money for a newly-married couple.

The film still attracts a lot of Americans to the Cong area and it is pleasing here to see our own sons and daughters having video tapes of it and enjoying the story. I watch it a lot and it is interesting to look back on the village in those days and see some of the older landmarks which disappeared. You see Curran's pub as Victor McLaglen spits on his hand to clinch a sale in the cattle-fair scene and that was a very popular place and really *the* pub in Cong at that time but no longer exists. Quite a few of the old, thatched buildings in that part of the street were taken over when Ryan's Hotel was extended. Some people felt the film showed the Irish with rough eating habits, the way Maureen O'Hara served the potatoes in the farmhouse scene. But we all loved helping make the movie. I thought it showed up the scenery beautifully and it portrayed the people as being kind and homely which they surely are in this part of the world.

Lord Killanin:

I've always said the film was a western made in Ireland rather than an Irish film but it did more for Irish tourism and the country than anything else. It was not very popular here at first and there were strong objections to the line from May Craig: 'Here's a fine stick to beat the lovely lady,' a line I suspect Jack Ford wrote into the script.

Etta Vaughan went for afternoon tea to Ashford Castle and suddenly found herself in front of the movie cameras. She recalls:

I lived in the village of Moycullen near Galway and had heard about the film people being in Cong. With a few friends I went there for the day just to have a look around out of curiosity. While having tea at Ashford Castle I became aware that some people, speaking with American accents, were taking more and more interest in our table and staring in our direction.

In the Footsteps of *The Quiet Man*

One of the gentlemen got up and walked over towards us. Unknown to me at the time it was Wingate Smith, John Ford's brother-in-law. He quite brusquely asked me to 'stand up'. I refused. He then said he would like me to be stand-in for Maureen O'Hara. I was completely taken aback. Apparently more than a hundred girls had applied for the job. I told him I would have to ask my mother's permission and he wore an incredulous look, not believing that a girl in her 20s would have to speak to her mother. But this was Ireland and I would do nothing like that without permission. I came from a happy but disciplined family and I adored my parents. My mother agreed but said she did not want me staying in Cong. Republic Pictures agreed that I could stay in Galway and with a fleet of limousines on hire from Dublin, they were happy to send a car for me every day and take me home in the evenings after work.

My very first day on location brought me some real blushes. They were shooting the holy water font scene and during a break one of my friends came over and said: 'Would you ever introduce me to John Wayne?' The only actor I recognised was Barry Fitzgerald who was such a lovely, comical person. I had hardly ever been to the cinema let alone seen a western and, not wishing to admit my ignorance, I made an excuse, left my friend, walked up to this tall good-looking man and asked: 'Would you be good enough to point out Mr John Wayne?' 'I'm John Wayne,' he said in that drawl. I almost collapsed with embarrassment but he took it all very well and was charming. In fact, the story swept the whole area and became the great joke of the week. A while afterwards, when I had got to know him quite well, I said: 'John, I was horrified, mea culpa, mea culpa.' He just laughed when I told him I had never seen a western.

He had a fine sense of humour and my favourite memory is of the day we were all heading out in trucks and vans to Maam Valley and the White O'Mornin' cottage for a full day's work. It was very warm and John Ford, as ever, was at the head of the convoy. John Wayne said to me: 'Let's go into that little pub for a quick one. The chief will never know.' I declined but three others joined him. They emerged a few minutes later roaring with laughter. For whatever reason, every glass in the

Looking like a star: Maureen O'Hara and stand-in, Etta Vaughan

pub had been smashed the previous night and they had been served their porter in jamjars. This really tickled John who talked and laughed about it for days afterwards.

I must say I was also impressed by his two sons, Patrick and Michael. The boys were up at the crack of dawn every morning and served Mass before work started. The Catholic church is still in the same place, just across the road from the house which was used as the Playfair home, but you would not recognise it now because the old sloping roof had to be removed and replaced by a flat one but at least the Clarke window was preserved and moved to ground level right behind the altar. I was lucky to make friends with a number of the cast and people like May Craig and Eileen Crowe were wonderful. Eileen went on to Hollywood for the interior shots and always kept in touch by letter.

There was a great friendship and comradeship about the filming, and the actors and actresses, even when not personally involved in a particular scene, would turn up to watch and lend support. Some would pull on Connemara shawls and move about in the background and have a good laugh. There was a great sense of fun about everything.

John Ford was always very kind and he had the total respect of his staff who would await him at the Ashford reception area each morning, click their heels, salute and say: 'Good morning chief.' He sometimes wore a snazzy little hat with a feather on the side. One day he suggested I should maybe go back to Hollywood and look for some work in the movie industry. I thanked him for his offer and said, although it was all an incredible experience, it was not something I would want to pursue. I felt I was growing up overnight, dealing with these high-powered Americans. I had been thrown into an exciting world from a rather reserved background and I couldn't get used to the thousands of people coming and going and those who gawked at me and actually asked for my autograph simply because as a mere stand-in, I was in front of the cameras. 'What must it be like for the stars themselves,' I thought. I told John Ford: 'I love where I live, I love my walks, my garden and I love watching things grow.'

I suppose in those days I was a lady of some leisure as I had left my schooldays well behind me and didn't work. My family were comfortably off and times were happy. However, the 60 pounds a week I got from Republic was very welcome. Another of the cast I loved was Ward Bond. He was a lovely gentleman and we had great fun. He would say to me: 'Little red-head, I'll take you back to America with me.' And I would reply: 'I'm no good at all to you, after all you've been married twice.' I was greatly impressed the day he did the fishing scene on the Cong River with Maureen O'Hara. His acting was superb and he displayed all the professionalism of a real fisherman, which he was. It was one of his great passions and he would always be away with his rod between scenes.

Funnily enough the one person I could not get close to was the lady I stood in for – Maureen O'Hara. She wasn't very outgoing towards me in those days. She had left home at an early age and was very much in the limelight. I often wondered if, because of her circumstances, being very highly paid, she was materialistic. Perhaps it was the pressure of work, personal problems or the impersonal lifestyle of being in one place one day and in another the next. It must be a tough, demanding life and it was perhaps summed up one morning when her little daughter, who was seven at the time, came running downstairs at Ashford Castle shouting: 'Mummy! Mummy!' and threw her arms around me, mistaking me for her mother. All the travelling and the long hours must have been hard on them both. However, I was to meet Maureen again many years later when she was honoured with a doctorate at Galway University and she had become very mature and sweet. She could not have been nicer to me.

I always remember how scenes had to be rehearsed time and again. I had to go on the tandem with Joe Mellotte till they got all the angles worked out, then on the horse and trap. We went up and down the street heaven knows how many times. I also had to run across the little stream at the cottage and got soaked. Then Maureen would take over for the close-up shots. We, of course, wore the exact same clothes so as I could do a lot of the long shots. We had similar figures and you would never have been able to spot the difference. Maureen was extremely talented and did her own singing and piano

Maureen O'Hara pulls on a Connemara shawl to join in the fun – as does stand-in, Etta Vaughan! May Craig (left) has her hand on the shoulder of John Wayne's wife, Chata, while he and the extras look on

playing in the White O'Mornin' scenes. She had a beautiful voice.

One of the most tiring scenes was at the Ashford farmhouse, the Danaher house, when they shot Maureen crying at the window as her suitor left empty-handed. It was a brief scene in the film but I had to sit under sweltering lights for hours and then Maureen stepped in. It was only right that the star be spared the gruelling part because she was so important to the film. But she had to be up early in the mornings and work very, very hard. It might have been a glamorous existence but it is one I did not envy her.

Mary Farragher lives in the 'Danaher' home as she did in 1951. The Ashford farmhouse has a plaque on the wall stating simply: 'Quiet Man House – 1951.' The house originally belonged to the Guinness family who leased it to her late husband's parents who, in turn, were permitted to pass it on to their son. The only change today is a small porch at the front door. Mary recalls:

Although I didn't take part in the film I probably had one of the best views. They were here in the farmyard for about a week. I would carefully peek out from behind the curtains upstairs and I remember watching as John Wayne, clutching a posy of flowers, approached with Barry Fitzgerald.

My biggest task was to keep my two young children quiet. My husband Peter and I, plus May who was six and Paul, just 18 months, had to live upstairs during that week of filming even although all of the shots were exterior. The interior of the Danaher house was a studio set in Hollywood. All of the interior scenes were shot there except when you see Maureen O'Hara looking through the window just to the left of my door.

I got a chance to speak to all of the stars during breaks and they were all very nice. Maureen O'Hara has been back here a few times on visits and come round to the farmyard. The last time she appeared I was outside tending to some flowers. She was showing friends around the various film locations and was charming to me, saying how nice it was to see me again. She looked marvellous and obviously has a great affection for the place and for the movie as she has come back to Ashford

Plaque on the Ashford farm buildings

The Danaher house in Ashford farmyard: the only change since 1951 is the addition of the porch

Castle just about every year since. She was a beautiful girl, very photogenic.

Two other scenes I can vividly recall were also shot out in front of the house. There was Barry Fitzgerald in his matchmaking outfit, top hat, black coat and all, and then the start of the big fight which began along there in the threshing field. When I look out of the kitchen window I swear I can still see Barry standing there as though he was plastered with the drink, rocking backwards and forwards on his heels. You would have sworn he was drunk as a lord when he slurred 'Thon Shornton' and did all that bit about the party of the first part and the party of the second part. He was, without doubt, the most comical of men, a great actor who practically stole the whole show. Everybody loved him. The threshing field starts at the gable of the house just along from us and is recognisable because of its slope even though it's a bit overgrown these days. There was a terrific crowd for that scene and it was all very exciting.

We never got a penny for our inconvenience of having to live upstairs but to be honest we just enjoyed the experience. The cash probably went to Mr Huggart who owned the land.

Jack Murphy, owner of 'Cohan's Bar':

My father was paid 600 pounds by Republic Pictures for the use of the place over a four-week period and for putting up the Cohan sign. There wasn't a lot of money about the place in those days although people got by and were happy. It was enough for him to buy a bit of farmland and they were good enough to let him open for business if they finished early for the day.

Although to this day the sign above the door states ' Pat Cohan – Bar', like my father I don't sell drink, just the usual things you find in a general store. It was a great location for them, being at the bottom of a steep hill. Apart from my involvement in the fight scene I had a station-wagon and drove a lot with the second-unit cameras so I was all over Connemara and at places like Clifden and Tully Cross where the horse-race scene took place on the beach. These were mainly the long-distance shots in which the stand-ins could be used saving time and money.

The film created work for so many people, not just the extras. Technicians, mainly brought in from London, filled the local Ryan's Hotel and guest houses. Local tradesmen were employed, some using their skills to make celtic crosses and headstones out of hardboard so we could carry them about for different scenes. The shops did well because, with it being just after the war, many things were still rationed although in Ireland the likes of tinned fruit and chocolate were plentiful and the visitors bought up everything to post home in parcels.

Mary Gibbons:

They bought and they bought. They bought up practically the whole area. They would go to Westport and elsewhere and buy up bed linen, towels and nylon stockings which were still scarce in Britain. If they were going to a remote location spot they would even leave money with the locals to buy things for them when supplies arrived.

Jack Murphy:

Mind you, the money ran dry for the few American technicians at one stage. Randolph Turpin was fighting the great Sugar Ray Robinson and the Yanks were offering 10–1 and were taken to the cleaners when Turpin won the World Middleweight title on points. They were cleaned out and in very bad form about it.

Robert Foy:

The scenes were incredible. Every morning about six a.m. a huge convoy of trucks and CIE buses containing all types of equipment, generators, costumes, dressing-rooms, mobile toilets and the rest would stretch half a mile as it snaked its way to the location sites. It was an early rise but some days you could be lucky in that they just wanted you for a short time. Whether you did just a couple of hours or the whole day, the money was the same.

In the Footsteps of *The Quiet Man*

Michael Hopkins:

> The great thing about it was that we were paid cash up front at the end of each day's filming. Times were pretty hard and money scarce and there was a lot of emigration to England and America. There were a couple of hundred of us working as extras at one time or another and it was a great boost to the area. My wage was £1 4s a week and here were the film people giving me £1 10s a day.

Robert Foy:

> On top of the cash, they would provide us each day with a boxed lunch from Ashford Castle which, even in those days, cost 12/6d. That was a real perk and very nice too.

Jack Murphy:

> I was just a lad of about 17 at the time and simply happy to be a part of such excitement. I'll never forget the fight scene in which I took part. It all began with John Wayne dragging Maureen O'Hara from the train and the station and then across fields. The locations were well spread out with the station at Ballyglunin being used and also the grounds of Ashford Castle. It took five days for that sequence.

Some 30-odd miles from Cong stands Ballyglunin Railway Station, virtually in the middle of nowhere and, just off the road between Tuam and Athenry, a very peaceful spot. It was there, just a month before filming had got under way, that Margaret Niland, her husband, Thomas, and their large family – they eventually had eight children – had moved into the two small rooms adjoining the waiting-room. Lord Killanin and John Ford had already visited the site and spoken to Mr Niland who had worked there for most of his life. This is where the opening scene of the train arriving in 'Castletown' would be shot.

'Castletown Station' at Ballyglunin

Front door of the waiting-room at 'Castletown Station'

In the Footsteps of *The Quiet Man*

Margaret Niland:

For reasons best known to themselves, they decided to change the name from Ballyglunin to 'Castletown' which I think is a place outside of Dublin. They came here every morning in cars, trucks and lorries. They were at it for two weeks yet in the film the station is seen for just a few minutes.

They would do little bits every day but to be honest, with so many children to look after and keep quiet, I didn't have much time to see what was going on. However my kitchen window, as it does today, looked on to the platform. I remember seeing Barry Fitzgerald outside the front door with his horse and trap and the poor man had to spend hours on end sitting on the edge of the little platform flowerbed waiting to be called. It must have been a pretty trying existence, as well as the bit of glamour attached to the job. They actually recorded the Irish songs used in the film out there in the waiting-room. With all the recording equipment already here, John Ford brought in a crowd of musicians and singers from the Irish Theatre in Galway and I could hear the likes of 'Wild Colonial Boy' booming all over the station.

While all of that was going on, the station was still open to the public but the waiting-room very much out of bounds. That made life difficult for my husband who had just two men to help him with the signal-box and the ticket office. He had to make sure the trains kept running and, unlike in the film, on time. It meant directing the trains down one track as the nearside one had been commandeered by the film unit. It was no easy task because there were up to eight passenger trains a day plus goods wagons to and from the old sugar-beet factory in Tuam which was busy at that time of year.

I think the story worked out well and the film has been good for tourism in Ireland. But, like many others at the time, I was furious when I looked out of the window and saw John Wayne dragging Maureen O'Hara from the train. And to this day I still don't like that bit where he drags her across the fields. That never happened in Ireland although the Americans seemed to think it did – and does. That scene is not so nice because I think it does the Irish down. But, to balance it, there is a lot of humour and how we all loved

Barry Fitzgerald. He was such a good actor, good person and a very humble man.

We get crowds, to this day, wanting to look around the station and we oblige. There's never a day goes by without cars rolling up and, although we get all nationalities, a huge number of the film's fans come from Northern Ireland. We get crowds of them down with their video cameras during July and it's nearly as busy as it was when the film was being made. CIE are keeping the place alive and have painted the station in the original colours of 1951. They have given permission to a private company to run special *Quiet Man* trains through here during the summer months. The carriages used in *The Quiet Man* were stock from the 1920 period in which the film was set. The special train running now is not that old but it is a steam train which gives the right atmosphere. It runs from Tuam to Athenry and stops off here to allow some photography. People tend to think the line has shut down but we are actually part of the main Limerick-Sligo line. Goods trains still run through here a few days a week and during the summer, on Sundays, there are pilgrims other than *Quiet Man* pilgrims with two, sometimes four, train-loads heading from Cork and Limerick to the shrine at Knock.

The old green, metal passenger-bridge across the track, seen in the film, is long gone. There used to be crowds on it watching some of the scenes being shot. It had been moved from Clifden to Ballyglunin around 1950 when Clifden Station was closed down. When the beet factory in Tuam closed, the bridge was dismantled again and moved from here to Ballinasloe, between Galway and Athlone, where it stands to this day. With the CIE lorries carrying more and more cement and manure, the station was allowed to run down. My husband, who died a couple of years ago, had retired in 1967 and regular services stopped two years after that.

The only other scene shot around here was quarter of a mile along the road to the right as you walk out of the station. That scene shows Michaeleen Oge Flynn driving Sean Thornton on the horse and trap as they go under a bridge with the train running overhead. Funnily, the train is on the same track as

101

Joe Mellotte

it was going into the station and in this shot is travelling in the opposite direction. But you can get away with anything in films I suppose. Anyway, it wasn't John Wayne or Barry Fitzgerald. I remember it was shot on a Sunday with their stand-ins used.

Joe Mellotte was Wayne's stand-in. To this day he is a celebrity, with many tourists flocking to his pub ('Mellotte's' of course) at the Neale, just a couple of miles from Cong, where he has a display of photographs taken during filming. Big Joe looks the part now as he did all those years ago. He is an imposing figure who gladly meets visitors and provides them with a quick lesson in historical semantics. Included in his repertoire is the story of the rapacious, once local landlord, Captain Boycott, whose tenants employed against him the strategy which now bears his name.

Standing in for John Wayne was just one of the roles in a varied life. Among his souvenirs are pictures of himself and Wayne plus more recent ones taken with President Ronald Reagan and John Travolta at Ashford Castle. When celebrities stay there Joe is invariably asked to attend. In his heavy brogue he recalls:

I was 27 at the time and fancied the part. I went along to see the Republic Pictures people and being six feet three I was lined up with about ten others of the same size and build. We had been chosen from hundreds of hopefuls. We stood in a line that morning and it was John Wayne himself who appeared, to carry out an inspection of the troops. He walked back and forward a couple of times, pointed at me and said in that drawl of his: 'That's him.' Then he disappeared as quickly as he had appeared. I had the job and at three pounds a day in the recessional fifties, I was a lucky man. That was twice the amount being paid to the extras.

I quickly discovered that if John Wayne wore a dark suit I wore an exact replica. If he had a blue shirt, so had I. Everything had to be identical and they even coached me in the famous Duke slouch. The first day I turned up for work he smiled and said: 'Welcome.' I did most of the risky scenes, including the famous horse-race scene on the beach. One of my main duties was to have 200 Camel non-filter cigarettes on me every day. He would go through virtually the lot asking for one about every five minutes although many had just a puff or two taken before being flicked away.

Although I was Wayne's stand-in I was also asked to crash through the door of Cohan's in place of Victor McLaglen at the climax to the fight scene. It was a nice soft landing because they had cushions on the street. The replacement doors were made of the thinnest plywood. It's amazing the illusions those film people can create.

Robert Foy:

There had been a much-publicised pact between John Ford and John Wayne that heavy drinking was out while the cast were in Ireland, although I understand they took quite a lot of the stuff while in Ashford Castle. I saw Wayne not able to stand up at times in the village and Ford would get very annoyed with him.

Wayne went off one day with the Irish professional heavy-weight champion 'Marching' Mairtin Thornton, some relation of Ford's from the Galway area. Thornton, because of the family ties, had kind of pushed himself on the movie crowd and, this particular day, he and Wayne disappeared into Connemara. They were only away a few hours but when they returned it was obvious that Thornton either hadn't been drinking as much as Wayne or was holding it better. Wayne was footless as he went into Ryan's Hotel right opposite my front door here. The next thing we heard was that Wayne wanted to fight Thornton, shouting only one would 'survive'.

Jim Fahy:

Thornton was heard to say: 'John, if I go to Hollywood will you see me all right?' 'Sure I will,' was the reply. 'Ah shit,' said Thornton. At this stage an English woman in the lounge reprimanded Thornton about his language and said: 'You mustn't speak to Mr Wayne like that. He's a gentleman.' The next thing she was taking to her heels as Thornton lurched through the panel of a door trying to get at her. A short time later a message arrived from Ashford Castle with John Ford demanding Wayne's immediate return. But the reply, delivered in that famous drawl was: 'You can tell Mr Ford that Duke is having a damned good time here in Cong.'

Robert Foy:

Just when it looked as though the two of them would fight, some film technicians intervened and, right on cue, Ward Bond and a few others arrived from Ashford Castle and bundled Wayne into a car.

Joe Mellotte:

Wayne had a few arguments with his mentor, Ford. As an actor he was a perfectionist and if a scene wasn't shot first time to his satisfaction he would get very angry. But he was never an arrogant man. He was the same in real life as he was in the movies. Everyone liked him. He had a great way with people. There's no doubt he preferred life in America to life in Ireland though he really enjoyed his stay. He would often give hints of his preference by saying just about everything was bigger and better in America.

The Extras Cast

Robert Foy:

John Wayne had been very amused to learn that electricity hadn't yet arrived in Cong. So when it did, towards the end of his stay, he made a big night of it in one of the pubs as the paraffin lamp went out for the last time and the Electricity Supply Board switch took over from the tinder box. Another night, some of the cast and crew had a large marquee erected beside the village hall and they had a huge celebration which included almost drinking O' Reilly's pub dry!

There's no doubt that the fight scene looked realistically good on film — as though they were giving each other a shellacking — but when you saw it being made close up it really was one big phoney. The fists were never nearer than eight or nine inches off the target. Victor McLaglen was a big, broad man with a boxing background but he got a bit of advice from his son, Andrew, an assistant director, who was around six-foot eight tall. I remember him saying: 'Dad, you're telegraphing your punches.' That was quite something to a man who had been a prize fighter in his day. It was said at the time, in fact, that the previous day Ford had cursed McLaglen, the mildest of men, in front of Andrew and blasted him for a poor performance.

Lord Killanin:

This was another example of Jack Ford trying to elicit a peak performance from the actor. He would also goad Duke Wayne and even have a go at Maureen O'Hara despite being friendly with both. In McLaglen's case the actor raged all night at his humiliation and every time he threw a punch the following day it was probably Jack Ford's face he saw in front of him. This was not unlike Jack's tactics with McLaglen in *The Informer*.

Robert Foy:

I remember John Wayne arriving one evening on the banks of the Cong River and we were all assembled for the scene where he whacks Victor McLaglen into the water. There was no sign of McLaglen so Wayne disappeared into one of the mobile dressing-rooms and emerged a short time later in fine clothing which would have cost any of us a few months' wages. Still there was no sign of McLaglen and after half an hour of pacing up and down Wayne began to look agitated.

Suddenly he stooped down and lifted a large cow pat. He then looked at the assembly and, to our astonishment, plastered it all over his shirt and trousers. He then threw it back on the ground and began rolling on top of it. Next he tried to rip the clothing without too much success so he demanded a pair of scissors from a wardrobe assistant and began cutting away, including a tear in the trousers just above the knee.

It was just then that McLaglen arrived. He was the oldest member of the cast, just over 65 years of age. He walked into the river and began splashing water all over himself and Wayne, who had annihilated his clothing, did likewise. Then both emerged with arms draped around the other's shoulders. The evening was cool and the water cold and a production assistant stood on the river bank clutching a brandy for McLaglen. I think they were afraid that at his age something might happen to him and that he must be shielded from hardship as much as possible. I suppose he was past playing that type of physical, hard-man role because of its demands. He certainly didn't come flying through Cohan's door at the end of the fight. Probably the most genuine part of the fight scene is when an extra tries to separate Wayne and McLaglen. You see Wayne lift him with one hand and throw him on to a haystack. That poor fellow was a taxi driver from Dublin. You should have seen his face!

Jack Murphy:

The one member of the cast I got to know very well was Victor McLaglen. I had a few drinks with him here in the village and also in Tuam and Galway. He loved a pint of Guinness and he told me about his boxing days and the fight with Jack Johnson. He had also been over to Scotland to watch Benny Lynch retain his British, European and World flyweight titles in front of a 40,000 crowd at

Shawfield Park in 1937. He never lost his love for the fight game.

He was a powerful, big man, although by 1951 you could see he was beginning to decline physically. He could be a bit forgetful about his lines and he slowed down the film quite a bit at times. With me having the station-wagon I would drive him about after a day's filming and he'd love to go through to Tuam for a steak. He loved a good Irish steak or Irish stew which he maintained he couldn't get in Cong or even Ashford Castle! I would drive him and two of his cronies over to the Imperial Hotel in Tuam where there was a woman who would cook his steak to perfection for him.

Although he liked his drink there were no late nights and I would have to have him back at Ashford sharp. They were on location from six in the morning till at least six at night. They were hard, hard workers. Mr Ford himself was also an early bedder.

Etta Vaughan:

Victor McLaglen's son, Andrew, had a wonderful dedication and devotion to his father. He cared for him and saw he was looked after properly. Victor told me: 'Every night that big boy of mine comes up to my bed and says "goodnight dad" and gives me a kiss. But now Etta, you keep that under your hat because Andy wouldn't like it if I was telling these tales.'

Fred O'Connor today runs a general store and pub in Cong the exterior of which was used by John Ford for the cattle-fair scene. In those days it was run by his parents, Arthur and Emily O'Connor and it was his mother's name, put up as a prop, which can be seen in the movie. Unlike the Cohan sign, it has disappeared.

Fred O'Connor recalls:

I drove Mildred Natwick about during her free time and I would take her to auctions as far afield as Athenry because she was interested in antiques. She was very good to our young daughter and for years after she returned to America she would send gifts over at Christmas and birthdays. She was a real lady, a lovely person with no airs or graces. I remember her telling me she was of Norwegian origin.

Mary Gibbons:

Miss Natwick became a very good friend to us. Fred would take her here and there and she visited her friend Kate O'Brien, the novelist, in Clifden. One evening, when Fred brought her back to Cong he invited her into the family home for coffee. A number of the film technicians were staying with the O'Connors on a bed-and-breakfast basis and this day had eaten them out of house and home. Fred's wife, Vera, came to my door in a bit of a panic and I remember her saying: 'Would you ever have a bit of brown bread in the house. I've nothing left and Mildred Natwick is in for coffee.' We were still awaiting the electricity switch-on so it was all pot-oven bread which was superb. You just couldn't beat it. Well, Mildred Natwick fell in love with it and asked Fred's wife where she'd got it from. The next thing I knew, Miss Natwick was in my living-room and we became very friendly over the next few weeks.

When it was time for her to go back to Hollywood she called by and asked if I would bake her some brown bread. I was glad to oblige but the first attempt didn't quite work out the way I had planned so I made another. In the event, she took both and, a short time later, I received a lovely letter from her. I had given her my sister's phone number in New York and she also made contact. She told my sister what a lovely time she had enjoyed in what was her only trip to Ireland. She was a lovely, caring person.

Robert Foy:

My main scene in the film was driving the horse and cart which delivered Sean Thornton's giant bed to White O' Mornin'. We did the scene 16 times that day, back and forward across the stream till they got it absolutely right. I was so exhausted I thought I was going to fall off the bloody cart. They kept going on about the light, the clouds and God knows what else.

Victor McLaglen and Mildred Natwick, driven by Barry Fitzgerald

The little track leading up to the ruin of White O' Mornin' today

Lord Killanin:

> Jack Ford would come and stay with me at Spiddal for the weekends and he gifted me that big bed used in the marriage-night scene. If you look carefully in the film you'll see there are two different beds; the one brought across the stream by cart in Ireland and the one used in the studio mock-up of White O' Mornin' in Hollywood. It's a bit like the John Wayne saddle story. Jack's attitude towards any fussy 'continuity people' was that if these small details were noticed by the cinema public then it wasn't a good picture.

Robert Foy:

> While it was exciting to see a movie being made it also took a lot of the wonder out of it.

The Extras' Cast

Jack Murphy:

I had been a great film-goer up till then but I've got to admit
that what I saw disillusioned me a bit and I didn't go back to
the cinema for many a long day. It spoiled the mystery for
me. To be honest, I haven't watched *The Quiet Man* now
for years. I knew too many people in it who have passed
on and it would be too sad for me. I'd rather not see it
now.

Mary Gibbons:

It's true many of the locals have since died but I watch it
regularly. I must admit that for a while after seeing it made
I would go to the cinema and try to work out what scene
might have been shot when, whereas, before the Republic
experience, you just assumed that they had been done in
chronological order. There's no doubt it took some of the
magic away. However, it remains a fascinating film and I
have discovered that no matter how many times you watch
it, each viewing throws up some little thing you have never
noticed before.

Robert Foy:

I think a lot of the film's popularity is down to the performance
of Barry Fitzgerald, who, in a way, stars in a film within the
film. Every time you saw him he would make you laugh.
His horse, Napoleon, was trained and supplied to Republic
Pictures by a man named Daly from Lough Mask. A clever
animal it was too as it automatically pulled up outside Cohan's
and nodded its head.

Republic paid good money for the hire of animals and all
kinds of props. Prop man Ace Holmes lived up to his first
name in lining up everything needed, like the bed, a set of
pewter mugs, old barrels, a cot and the old 1920s Morris
bullnose car. It belonged to a cousin of a man named Bernard
O'Sullivan from Cornamon who was later to meet and marry
Etta Vaughan, Maureen O'Hara's stand-in. Maybe the little
car triggered off the romance.

A huge, smoking steamroller-type machine, which had been hired from Mayo County Council in Ballinrobe, was also used. It sat at the top of the threshing field where it had been towed overnight by Charles FitzSimons, Miss O'Hara's brother, who played Forbes in the movie. He had discovered the old machine and was determined John Ford include it in the scene. The director loved it because it was so much more graphic and believable than the little forge anvil thing into which John Wayne was to throw the dowry. FitzSimons and Lee Lukather also found the famous tandem used by Wayne and O'Hara.

Jack Murphy:

I'm always delighted to have a bit of crack with visitors and tell them my memories from those far-off days. There's no doubt that the movie has been good for the village. It was only after it was released that they started coming here in their thousands.

Robert Foy:

Thankfully it wasn't pig-in-the-parlour stuff and it is a film which appeals to people of Irish descent, no matter where in the world they may be. The Americans, Canadians and Australians are particularly hyper about it. I remember an American doctor coming to stay at Ashford Castle and he was desperate to meet anyone who had taken part in the film. He wanted to know where John Wayne had stood in a particular scene. When the general spot was pointed out he became agitated and demanded to know exactly where the right and left feet had been! The same man had the staff at the castle demented with his constant phone calls to reception checking the time of the in-house showing of the *Quiet Man* video which is five p.m. every night of the year.

I suppose people are so hyper about it because of their Irish ancestry and they see the film as a kind of portrait of what they believe Irish life to be. Scenes like the one where Wayne and O'Hara go off shopping to Castletown on the horse and trap and leave their cottage door wide open show what a trust and innocence the Ireland of those

112

White O' Mornin', just to the right of the new cottage

days had. There is certainly a great sentimentality about it.

Apart from the story of the American doctor, I remember another fellow phoning me from Omagh in Northern Ireland a few years ago and asking if he could travel down to see me. I was painting the front door when he arrived some days later and he told me he was a member of the John Wayne Appreciation Society in Omagh and he wanted every detail I could give him on the actor and the movie. I helped as much as I could and off he went. Then, two weeks later, he wrote to say the society was having a festival during which they would show the film and have a general discussion. He offered to take me and my wife to Omagh for a week, all expenses paid, if I would address them on my memories of 1951. But I didn't go.

I was contacted by him again to say that his society was in a position to buy the White O' Mornin' ruin and its land out in Maam Valley. So I made some inquiries for them. The cottage was owned in 1951 by a Walter and Brigit Joyce who had five sons and three daughters. They continued living there even during filming because the shots were all exterior. The

113

Joyce family made so much money from Republic films that they built a new house adjacent to the cottage, which was allowed to deteriorate. They later sold the entire site to a colonel from the British Army who used it on fishing trips but after his wife died he sold it to a man from California who is planning to return the old cottage to its former glory and make it a tourist attraction. There's no doubt that the various locations have become shrines to fans of the film. We've even had a Spanish television crew over here making a documentary about it. It's unbelievable, after all this time, that it retains so much popularity.

Mary Gibbons:

It was the most hectic spell of my life. Although the summer had been the best for years and very dry, clouds affected the light and caused problems. Telegrams of anything between 350 and 500 words would tell John Ford which film reels had been fine and which would have to be shot again. Despite being run off my feet it was all a once-in-a-lifetime experience.

Jack Murphy:

The Republic people were very lucky with the dry weather. Had they come in 1950 they would have been swept away by the rain and the summer of '52 wasn't much better. They actually had to call in the fire brigade to hose down the street for the cattle-fair scene.

Mary Gibbons:

Between the telephone calls and telegrams it was chaotic and eventually I had to get an assistant. It would be two a.m. before the telephone calls between the Republic office in Ashford Castle and Hollywood would slow down. But then the Americans would start calling back at three a.m. They said they wanted a 24-hour service and I had to have a phone bell installed in my bedroom. I would get to sleep around six a.m. and my assistant would take over. Remember, before all of this we had managed on one telephone line!

There was no provision in this country at that time for shooting indoor scenes and they could not process the film here either. So the day's filming was packaged up each evening and driven from Ashford Castle to Shannon Airport, a good two hours' drive away. One of the drivers was Paddy O'Donnell, mentioned in the film titles. He also had a non-speaking part as the railway porter and is, in fact, the first person you see in the film. He has since died but his daughter, not even born then, lives just along the road.

Robert Foy:

The American film people could be very harsh at times and overstep the mark. They would take over the whole street and become very pushy. Even the Garda had more or less to do what they were told. John Ford would have his cables and generators all over the place. I remember one local fellow coming up the road with a truck and the way they spoke to him he would have had to have gone via Dublin to get to the other end of the village. He jumped down from his cab and gave out stink to them saying he had paid his road tax and he demanded his right of way.

Mary Gibbons:

I'll never forget the final day's filming. We were used to the crew being on the road early but this particular day we were awakened by a commotion in the street right in front of the post office and O'Connor's shop. I looked out from my bedroom window and saw sheep and cattle milling about. A largish crowd was also starting to gather. I was due on duty at six a.m. so it didn't bother me too much.

The postman had just arrived to collect mail and looked as puzzled as I did as I joined him at the front door. As we watched, one of John Ford's friends, an Andy O'Malley from Westport, took it upon himself to start telling about half a dozen locals that they would have to move on because they were in the way of the cameras. The postman and I went upstairs to get a better view of the proceedings and, as we looked out from behind the curtains, Andy McLaglen shouted: 'Get back from those windows, get back!' And two very frightened people did just that. It was only afterwards when you thought about it you realised how timid you had been. Those were our windows and our streets and not all of us were being paid for inconvenience. Still, I suppose the film did help a lot of people.

I remember the suddeness with which it all ended. The last shots were taken about 11a.m. on 14 July yet Ashford Castle had been booked for three months from 1 June till 31 August and the telephone service booked with the Department of Posts and Telegraphs for the same period of time. We saw Maureen O'Hara lift the whip as she argued with John Wayne over the dowry and, after giving the horse a clip, the trap moved off along the street and that was the last we saw of her. John Ford sang out: 'Wrap it up,' and filming was officially finished in Ireland. By early afternoon Ford had left with Lord Killanin. Ward Bond was seen speeding off by car to catch a plane to America, Maureen O'Hara was on her way to Dublin and Barry Fitzgerald took the Curragh Line to Galway. People rushed in all directions for boats, trains and planes although John Wayne and Jack McGowran were last to leave, at a leisurely pace. They were so far ahead of schedule it was unbelievable. They had even managed to take a day off on 4 July to celebrate Independence Day.

My assistant and I, who had been rushed off our feet and forgotten what a good night's sleep was, then felt it the longest day of our lives. Suddenly all the glamour and excitement which had engulfed us and made Cong such a hub of activity for those six remarkable weeks was gone and the phones stopped ringing.

Chapter Seven
BACK IN THE USA

Three days after completing filming in Cong and having stayed at Maureen O'Hara's family home in Dublin, John Ford flew back to Hollywood on 17 July 1951. Despite fatigue brought on by work and the eight-hour time difference, he was back in action shooting *The Quiet Man* interior scenes so quickly that, by 3 August, they had what is called in the business 'a wrap'. John Wayne had returned to the States with morale sky-high knowing that he had given one of his best-ever performances despite the role being a difficult one for his style of acting. But he was modest enough to say to friends: 'That was a goddam hard script. Hell, for weeks I was just playing a straight man to those wonderful characters, and that was really hard.' That was his personal tribute to the likes of Barry Fitzgerald and the Irish players from the Abbey Theatre.

All of the cast, as they broke up following the Hollywood takes, seemed more than happy with their labours. Wayne, who was later to admit to his third wife, Pilar, whom he had met in Peru, that *The Quiet Man* was his favourite film of the 200-plus movies he made, had suffered just one disagreement with John Ford during the Hollywood end of filming and that came when, in the wedding-night scene, Maureen O'Hara – who also admitted it was her favourite of the 55 movies she made – bolted the door on her new husband. The script called for Wayne to throw a pair of boxing gloves on to the turf and log fire in the cottage but he thought it was all wrong for the story line. After an argument, Ford, using more than a few expletives, changed it so Wayne could, as he had done in so many westerns, kick the door in.

This is another example of how the script and scenes changed as the movie progressed, just as Barry Fitzgerald inserted the word 'Impetuous' when he witnessed the broken marriage-bed.

Maureen O'Hara also had a blazing row with Ford on the Hollywood set which she thought might cost her a fine career. She recalled:

> As part of the plot in getting John Wayne and I married in the movie, we shot the scene of me sitting in the cart at the race scene where my hat was to be left on the stick. Normally, any director dealing with a woman who has long hair would put the wind machine in front of her and blow all the hair backwards. But John Ford, and it wasn't till I saw it on screen afterwards that I realised what a master and genius he was, put the machine behind me and my hair was blowing forward and lashing across my eyeballs like a whip, almost cutting my eyes to shreds. I kept squinting and Ford stopped everything and shouted: 'What the ★ ★ ★ ★ are you doing, open you're so-and-so eyes.' By this time he and John Wayne had driven me mad and my temper lasts just so long and wouldn't last any longer. I put my hands on the side of the cart, leaned forward and said: 'What would a bald-headed son-of-a-bitch know about hair lashing across his eyeballs?' After that I thought: 'Oh my God what have I done?' And I sat there. I watched for what seemed like an eternity. He checked every pair of eyes and every face on the set and then laughed and everybody started roaring with laughter.

One other spark between stars and director came when Wayne and O'Hara end up courting in the local cemetery where they are caught in a thunder storm. This was another of the Hollywood studio scenes, originally scheduled to be shot on the cliffs of Moher, and through a series of takes and retakes Ford insisted that they became even more passionate in their embraces. By the time the rain had soaked them to reveal the straining flesh through the fabric of their clothing they could feel every line and curve in each other's bodies. Wayne was heard to drawl afterwards: 'Hell, Ford just wanted me to do all the things he wanted to do himself.'

In the main, though, Ford and his stars hit it off and there's no doubt the casting of John Wayne and Maureen O'Hara for what was only their second film together had proved to be sheer genius. With his film editor, Jack Murray, mentioned in the film's opening titles, Ford spent the rest of August and September assembling the movie and, on 2 October 1951, sent the following letter to Lady Killanin:

I apologise for any abrupt leave-taking at Shannon. I remember Michael going to the plane with me but I was all choked up at leaving our beloved Ireland and was afraid I would burst into tears, which I did on reaching my berth and thereupon fell fast asleep and woke up in New York. I don't recollect anything at all hardly.

It seemed like the finish of an epoch in my somewhat troubled life. Maybe it was a beginning. Can I still come back? Don't be surprised if I show up in the very near future. Galway is in my blood and the only place I have found peace. Hey, 'The Quiet Man' looks pretty good. Everyone here is enthused. I even like it myself. It has a strange humorous quality and the mature romance comes off well. I'm now in the throes of cutting and dubbing music. It is indeed the tough part, requiring particular attention to detail. I think the Irish may even like it.

Well the quiet men and women all send love and regards. They still have that faraway look in their eyes mirrored in green hills and brooks. The Duke is sitting opposite and says: 'Can I come back too.' I've corrected him – 'May I come back too!' Love and affection to all, Jack.

Lord Killanin's personal copy of the shooting script for Republic Pictures production 1912, *The Quiet Man*, dated 30 April 1951, shows just how much Nugent adapted the script and how much John Ford edited it as they were filming. Cuts and changes were made and probably many of them to satisfy Herbert Yates who demanded the movie be no longer than two hours. They explain many odd references in the final version which are otherwise rather obscure.

In one of the original drafts of April 1951, now housed at the Irish Film Institute in Dublin, Nugent gives his potted biographies plus a lovely humorous introduction which encapsulates the special relationship between the writer and director. When he mentions the opening titles and credits he states: 'Behind them will be a series of shots in and around Galway, which the director knows like the back of his hand – the same back of the hand which this writer would get if he risks suggesting the shots!' He calls for an opening scene with the train puffing along and a mother with a boy of about five and a little girl of four in a third-class compartment. The girl sits nearest the window and both children are more intent on looking at the tall man opposite than they are on the breathtaking scenery. Had the opening scene not been cut from the script, Sean Thornton's first line as he jerked his thumb towards the scenery would have been: 'Nice, real nice', followed by dialogue between himself and the mother. One tell-tale cut in the final edit comes when Thornton steps from the train at 'Castletown'. He turns back towards the compartment, pulls something from his pocket, holds it in the air and utters his first word: 'Thanks.' The object, if you look closely, is an apple. In the original script it has been given to him by the little boy. Similarly, at the station the script calls for an old woman carrying a basket of fish, a young man with a greyhound held tight to its leash, a few children scampering up to study the locomotive, porters trundling boxes and crates, and passengers boarding and alighting – quite different from the finished article. Instead of walking on to the platform and just lifting Thornton's luggage as he does in the movie, Michaeleen Oge Flynn, according to the script, tells each and every one of the railway staff what he thinks of them then takes the Yank to Innisfree. Again, once en route they stop, not on the little hump-back bridge seen in the movie, but on a hillcrest as they view White O' Mornin'. There's no mention of the line: 'That's nothing but a wee, humble cottage,' indicating that Ford and Barry Fitzgerald ad-libbed throughout the film.

However, in the original script there is much earlier mention of Red Will Danaher's intentions towards the Widow Tillane. Likewise, when Father Peter Lonergan walks into shot for the first time and asks for a private word with Michaeleen, it emerges in the script that the parish priest is a gambler on the horses, and Flynn, apart from being the *shaughraun* – the marriage-broker – is also the village bookmaker. He tells Lonergan that his betting arrears stand at £3 8s 6d now that 'Mad Hatter' has also lost. In the movie, the discussion is private and no details disclosed. In the script the priest then blasts the horse for going wide on the far

PRODUCTION #1912

"THE QUIET MAN"

by

Maurice Walsh

Screenplay

by

Frank Nugent

1. MAIN TITLE. BEHIND the TITLE and the CREDITS there will be
a series of shots in and around Galway, which the director
knows like the back of his hand -- the same back of the hand
which this writer would get if he risked suggesting the
shots.

OVER THE TITLE AND CREDITS will be heard a soft Irish bari-
tone singing ~~~~~~~~~~~.

FADE IN:

2. EXT. THE GALWAY-CLIFDEN TRAIN: (DAY) LONG

This is a "~~~~~~~," picturesque little train which follows
a causeway and can be silhouetted against the sky. It has
a ~~~ whistle, an interesting driving shaft and a puffing
stack; and it whistles, drives and puffs all in rhythm with
a gay and lilting tune.

3. INT. THIRD CLASS COMPARTMENT OF SAME TRAIN: MED. CLOSE

On a MOTHER with a boy about 5 and a little girl of 4. The
little girl sits nearest the window. The youngsters have
no eyes for the passing scenery, but are staring with the
innocent and unabashed fascination of children at the man
who sits opposite.

4. INT. THIRD CLASS COMPARTMENT OF TRAIN: ANGLE

On SEAN THORNTON, as he scans every detail of the passing
countryside with kindling eyes and a happy smile.

(Sean Thornton is in his late thirties, a big man with a
light tread, an easy smile and the gift of silence. His
biography can be briefly written. Born in Inisfree, he
was fatherless at 4. An uncle in America sent for the mother and himself. She died when he was 12. From that time
forward he had to fend for himself -- newsboy, sweeper, lab-
orer, stoker, steel puddler, boxer, contender, near-champ-
ion and then -- killer of a man in the prize-ring. A different killing this than in the war in which Sean had served. So "Trooper" Thorn hung up his gloves, counted his ring-
earnings and bethought himself wistfully of his mother's
somewhat-idealized recollections of their native Inisfree.
Now to Ireland he is returning, a Quiet Man seeking forget-
fulness of all the wars of the human spirit.) •

Sean turns and his smile becomes embarrassed before the un-
winking stares of the children. His thumb jerks at the
scenery.

CONTINUED:

jf

Shooting script

turn and blesses himself by way of an apology. Unrepentant about his little vice, however, Lonergan decides to put half a crown on Ard-Ri in the steeplechase, then ups it to a crown.

Meanwhile Thornton starts eating his apple and spots Mary Kate Danaher for the first time. In the movie, he lights one of his many cigarettes. She jumps over a wall and returns his smile with a greeting in Gaelic which, translated, means 'a bright good day to you'. With that, she and her herd of sheep are off. The script, which runs to 146 pages, quotes Lonergan, who is carrying his trout rod and a dozen or so fishing flies, as thanking Thornton for coming to Mass, saying it might encourage others to attend chapel occasionally. This is a direct dig at the listening Michaeleen who exacts instant retribution by telling the priest that Ard-Ri has lost and that Mrs Playfair, the wife of his Church of Ireland counterpart, has backed the winner!

As the script progresses, the hunting-style man leaning on the mantlepiece of the Widow Tillane's sitting-room as Thornton and Danaher bid for White O' Mornin' is referred to as 'Captain Guppy', a would-be gentleman who has hopes of ultimately winning Mrs Tillane and her considerable property. She introduces him (actor Don Hatwell) as her English-accented land agent, but his only actual mention in the film comes during the race scene when one of the elderly judges, watching through binoculars, shouts: 'Foul, Guppy.' Tillane's midget maid, played by Elizabeth Jones, one of Ford's 'Repertory Company', who opens the door to introduce Danaher – 'wipe your muddy boots' – is referred to in the script as 'Nell'. The five men at Danaher's kitchen table are described as his farmers – not family – and the one who talks about Thornton's father 'having shoulders like an ox' is the Packy McFarlane whom Danaher refers to in his early meeting with Tillane.

Thornton, after walking with Michaeleen to spend his first night at White O' Mornin', spots Mary Kate hiding behind some shrubbery rather than finding her in the cottage. There is also a lot more of Thornton's mother's voice heard in the shooting script. Two other changes see Tobin's line go from: 'I do not believe I heard your name young man' to '*tall man*' and Michaeleen's: 'Ah, it is a full soft moon so I'll away to me comrades and talk a little treason before I turn in,' to 'Well it's a fine soft night so I think I'll go and join me comrades and talk a little treason. Good night

Sean, God bless you,' — one of the few political references in the whole movie. Also, in the script Mrs Playfair is in the driving seat of the tandem with her husband on the back reading a book while in the movie the roles are reversed.

An entire scene building up to the horse race was omitted because of the running time. It took place in Cohan's bar with the names of the horses, Minotaur, Shiny Posy, Danny Boy and Fingal, the latter two owned by Danaher and Tillane, displayed on a betting board. Feeney is to ride for Danaher and Guppy for Tillane, and there is plenty of dialogue with Mrs Playfair embarrassing her husband as she relates the tale of how she once put up her bonnet for him in a three-legged race which he won! She adds to his severe discomfort by saying: 'Cyril hopped and skipped like a man possessed.' Thornton then appears on the scene and pays the one guinea entry fee for his horse, Black Jack, which he insists on riding himself, prompting Danaher's decision that he too will do his own riding despite his considerable bulk. Because of the cuts, dialogue had to be used to link into the race scene. Another change meant Sean and Mary Kate emerge from church rather than the Danaher house to start their famous courting scene. When the courting couple run away from the watchful eye of Michaeleen he gives chase, just as in the movie, and the horse pulls up abruptly outside Cohan's. A surprised proprietor, looking out from an upstairs window, utters: 'It's Sunday, we're closed.' Michaeleen, as ever desperate for a drink, replies: 'Sure I know that but the horse doesn't.' In the movie the scene ends with the horse stopping at the pub door.

The wedding scene is considerably longer in the original script which also shows a completely different setting for Mary Kate's meeting with Father Lonergan when she unburdens her troubles. In the movie, it takes place on a river bank while the priest stalks a salmon, but the intention had been to shoot the scene in church, St Anseln's, in a confessional. The plan was a studio scene with a tripartite confessional and a few pews in the immediate foreground. As the exasperated priest slams one grill shut on Mary Kate he opens the other one only to be confronted by the face of Michaeleen who tells him 'Mad Hatter' is running again at Punchestown. The other grill is also slammed!

Other changes come when Michaeleen asks Cohan for his parabellum (revolver) and the proprietor looks around covertly

Courtesy of Irish Film Institute

The magical moment Maureen O'Hara makes her entrance

before going to a wooden collection box on the wall marked 'hospital fund'. The script then calls for Thornton to drag Mary Kate through a stream with her shoes on and there is much more dialogue between Widow Tillane and Mrs Playfair during the fight scene as they observe through binoculars. The fight spills past the church and the chief protagonists take time to bless themselves when they realise where they are and the chasing crowd all tip their hats as they pass by. Tobin is carried out of the house in his bed waving a stick and shouting 'Up the rebels!' In the movie he runs from the house still pulling on his trousers having leapt from his death bed! Thornton and Danaher come crashing through the pub door together and the fight continues till Danaher makes one last rush and Thornton stops him with a left, sinks a right across into his belly, straightens his head with a left upper cut and then drives a short, merciful right flush on to the button of his chin. With that Thornton steps back, and the crowd hushes for just a moment, Danaher's eyes glaze, he sways like a giant tree then he falls forward full length and doesn't even quiver when he hits the ground. Michaeleen desperately shouts at Danaher to get up or he, Flynn, will be ruined as a bookmaker.

That original shooting script can be viewed by making an appointment with the very helpful staff at the Irish Film Institute, 6 Eustace Street, Dublin, just a few minutes walk along the south bank of the Liffey from O'Connell Street. It is certainly an eye-opener in terms of how a movie can change so much as filming progresses.

While those final touches were being put to the movie, Herbert Yates came up with another outrageous title, *The Prizefighter and the Colleen*. He moaned, even at this late stage, that a script about an ex-fighter and an Irish girl would not sell tickets at the box office and after seeing the film in rough-cut he again said it was not commercial and insisted on cuts neither Ford nor Merian C. Cooper could accept. Charles FitzSimons is now Executive Director of the prestigious Producers' Guild of America having produced more than 300 hours of television and theatrical

It was from this doorway that Francis Ford ran to witness the big fight

motion pictures. He recalled at his home in Berwick Street, Los Angeles:

> Herb Yates was a Scotsman – he told me that himself in a private moment one day. He was a short man with a real Scottish face although where he got the Herb from I don't know. He was a typical Hollywood mogul and guarded every cent which I suppose he was entitled to do with his own money. I suppose the best way to sum him up is as a funny despot. He had a beautiful little Spanish-style one-storey executive office-block, part of which was shared by John Ford and Merian Cooper, and it had a winding path through a lovely lawn to his personal entrance. Herb being Herb, he had restricted the use of the parking space and forbidden anyone to walk on his lawn. I would visit Ford often and one day Herb came bursting in, pointed a finger at me and shouted: 'You've parked in my space.' Ford distracted him and they got talking about something else. Then, as Herb left, obviously having forgotten which mortal sin I'd committed, he shouted: 'You walked on my lawn.'
>
> I remember in Ireland Ward Bond climbed to the top of an old ruin of a tower in the grounds of Ashford Castle and scraped on the inside wall: 'F ★ ★ ★ Herb Yates.' Then in a roundabout way he got someone to tell John Wayne about the spectacular view to be had from the tower. Wayne swallowed the bait and his face was priceless when he saw the message in such an unlikely spot. He came back roaring and laughing when he realised the joke that had been played on him. He laughed himself silly.
>
> Wayne, Bond and Victor McLaglen were, of course, giants of the industry and giants in every sense. They were card-playing buddies and strong men with strong personalities. So you can tell that Herb Yates was not the most popular man in the world with the cast. He had been used to shooting 70-minute movies so he though *The Quiet Man* was incredibly over length. But Merian Cooper insisted they had a deal and they must stick to it.

John Wayne's contract with Republic Pictures was about to expire and he decided to tell Yates what to do with the new one on offer. He could put up with the studio owner in terms of his own career but the way the Republic chief had treated his friend and mentor, Ford, proved too much for Wayne to take. Much to Yates's surprise Wayne walked out and formed his own production company, Wayne-Fellowes, and became one of the first big film stars to do so. Almost immediately, he signed a ten-film contract with Warner Brothers at $150,000 a time plus ten per cent of the profits. Not bad for a bit-player who had started at $75 a week, although he would go on to command $600,000 and more per picture at the height of his career.

Back at Republic, the long-suffering John Ford had fortunately fought off the suggested title change by Yates although when Yates saw what was to be Academy Award-winning photography of the beautiful Irish scenery by Winton Hoch he complained that it was 'all green'! Again he insisted that the film must be cut and on 16 October sent the following memo to Ford: 'My experience has taught me that audiences, no matter how good a picture is, do not want any picture to run over two hours. Exhibitor reaction is the same. In fact Loew's will not play a picture running over two hours and this is true of other important first-run theatres.' Ford, meanwhile, as he had told Lady Killanin, was scoring the film with Irish songs like 'Isle of Innisfree' which had been written by a Dublin policeman, Richard Farrelly, and was totally suited in that its theme was of an emigrant searching for the peace and tranquillity of home. It was adapted by Ford, Charles FitzSimons and Maureen O'Hara. Retired Garda Sergeant Farrelly, a native of Kells, Co. Meath, died in August 1990. He had served at Dublin Castle, the Garda headquarters. Old favourites like 'Wild Colonial Boy' and 'Galway Bay' were joined by 'The Young May Moon' and 'The Humour is On Me Now', taking *The Quiet Man* to the verge of a musical – certainly the nearest thing to one which John Ford had ever made. He would send for music of the period when doing his research and always entered his office for meetings well armed with a miscellany of fact and fancy to toss casually at the writer, wardrobe man or anyone else who fell under the spell and the gleam of his celtic eye.

As the film was nearing completion, there was a real buzz around the Republic lot that something special was on the go, that Ford had another masterpiece on his hands. Anyone who saw the rough stages reckoned it was a winner, except, of course, Yates, who was still insisting on 120 minutes. Ford had cut out whole sequences but it was still running at 129 minutes. Yates, out to make sure he covered his costs, decided to show the finished article in private to some Republic executives and distributors, thinking that if they turned it down, he would publicise the fight scene, get some interest going and then quickly shunt it out via mass distribution in the hope of retrieving his investment before public opinion could cause any real damage to the movie's reputation. Charles FitzSimons recalled: 'Herb Yates had no confidence in the movie right up until the last minute and he actually opened it at New York's Capital Theatre with a midweek date and threw in a supporting stage-show to attract an audience.' Meanwhile, John Ford kept playing for time and managed to keep his version away from Yates. He kept it under wraps till the actual private screening and then pulled a masterstroke.

The audience was obviously enthralled by what was on offer but suddenly, after exactly 120 minutes, the screen went blank. When Yates demanded an explanation Ford said he had cut out the fight scene. The executives and distributors demanded to see more and Ford switched the movie back on – fight scene and all. As they all applauded at the end, a smiling Yates accepted Ford's 129-minute version. And, after tapping public opinion at the New York venue, the Republic mogul realised he was on the verge of making a fortune. His attitude changed completely and from loathing the movie he loved it. He then mounted the studio's biggest-ever publicity campaign and booked *The Quiet Man* into the Radio City Music Hall – the only Republic Picture ever screened there at that time. The telegrams and memos began flying as excitement mounted:

25 October 1951 – Ford to Lord Killanin: ' "The Quiet Man" looks good. If you are still talking to Huggard [the owner of Ashford Castle who loathed the film people and who was toasted each evening by them as Huggardy Buggerdy] which I am not, you might tell him that the tourist board may expect an influx of film companies this next 18 months.'

3 December 1951 – Ford to Killanin: 'The Quiet Man looks better and better. There is a vague possibility that even the Irish will like it.'

7 February 1952 – telegram from Yates to Ford: 'While the Music Hall will give the picture great prestige throughout the world, nevertheless we will not be disappointed if we have to pre-release

The Quiet Man in another theatre here as every important theatre in Broadway is bidding for the picture with extended runs.'

A short time earlier a Republic executive, J. R. Grainger, sent Ford a strong memo telling him that it was wrong for John Wayne's image to be in a film entitled *The Quiet Man* and it should be changed. A little later the same man was sending a memo to Yates telling him what an outstanding success the film had become!

17 February 1952 – telegram from Yates to Ford re another private screening of the movie: 'Had you been here you would have gone home ten years younger.'

April 1952 (undated) — letter from Mrs Francis Ford to John Ford: 'He [Francis] hasn't worked for almost a year. Wish you could help him. He walks the floor constantly.'

12 April 1952 – message from top UK film critic, Lindsay Anderson, to Ford after seeing the trade screening: 'The film relaxes as it delights. We all in Britain admire the dynamism of American film-making but how much more satisfying in the end is this kind of strength which can afford to pause or just meander along instead of beating audiences about the head. I think you've succeeded completely.'

6 May 1952 – memo from the Republic executive committee re the Spanish title for the film: ' "El Hombre Callado" would be a mistake as its connotation in Spanish is quite different. If possible we should get the word "Amor" into the title.'

12 May 1952 – The Hollywood Reporter *and* Variety *reviews were published*. The *Reporter* stated: ' "The Quiet Man" is a heartwarming, tender comedy drama of nostalgia which reflects the directional genius of John Ford.' *Variety* said: 'John Ford's "The Quiet Man" is a charming, often whimsical, sometimes brawling piece of entertainment.'

27 May 1952 – Cinematographer Winton C. Hoch to Ford: 'Thank you for the pleasure of working on "The Quiet Man".'

July 1952 (undated) – London Republic office telegram to Yates re "The Quiet Man": 'Excellent box office here.'

6 September 1952 – telegram from Yates to Ford re reaction to The Quiet Man *at the Venice Film Festival*: 'Thunderous ovation. Audience consisted of three thousand persons in formal dress from every free country. It was a sight I do not ever expect to see again.' Can this be the same Herbert Yates?

September 1952 also saw *The Quiet Man* company dinner at which there were presentations to Ford, Cooper and Yates.

14 September 1952: telegram from Yates to Ford telling him the film has scooped three awards at the Venice Film Festival.

25 September 1952 – letter from Dublin policeman, Richard Farrelly to Ford re the use of his song 'Innisfree': 'It has been the means of bringing me the break I have been looking for all these years and to my people and myself that has been the cause of great joy.'

29 September 1952: letter from Ford to Lord Killanin suggesting they do another Maurice Walsh story from *Green Rushes – Bad Town Dublin* – for a new film company they are planning to set up, Four Province Films, an Irish company.

6 October 1952 – letter from Yates to Bruce Newbury, Republic Pictures, London office re Ford's trip to Britain: 'Send three dozen roses to Claridges with card reading "Dear Mary, welcome to London. You have a joyous holiday – Herb Yates."'

6 October 1952 – letter from Yates to Jack Clement, Republic Pictures office, Paris: 'Send three dozen beautiful roses with card "Dear Mary, welcome to Paris . . ."'

6 October 1952 – letter from Yates to Henry Lombroso, Republic Pictures office, Rome: 'Send three dozen beautiful roses . . .'

6 October 1952: letter from A. W. Perry to Yates saying *The Quiet Man* was a success in Canada.

13 January 1953 – letter from Yates to Ford: 'Every paper I pick up from all parts of the country all pick "The Quiet Man" as best picture. No doubt you will get an Oscar. You probably know that Wayne spent four or five days in Acapulco and is now on his way to Brazil. I wonder who he's chasing or who is chasing him.'

Undated – letter on Wayne-Fellowes paper from John Wayne to Ford re his divorce from Chata: 'The $150,000 they asked for attorneys' fees and investigation and appraisers and court costs was cut to $20,000. Her $9,000 a month was cut to $1,100 a month cash and $1,400 a month maintenance of the house. So I guess I can say I won a moral victory. Those are capital dollars we're talking about, not tax dollars.'

Meanwhile *The Quiet Man* went from strength to strength with reviews heaping praise upon Ford and his stars. The box office boomed across the States and queues formed everywhere with people returning time and again to see it. Just about every cinema manager wanted to hold on to the precious reels for extended runs, some for up to two months.

Yates wallowed in the role of 'creative genius' as Hollywood papers tipped *The Quiet Man* for Academy Awards. But John Ford was so sickened by his experience with Yates that he just wanted to walk away from his great triumph. It had been his project. He had found and nurtured the story yet Yates was now sharing in the glory. While the ballyhoo was in full swing Ford decided that his relationship with Yates must be terminated as quickly as possible and he contacted Lord Killanin again about their intended Irish film company.

It was in his last film for Yates, *The Sun Shines Bright*, set in a Kentucky town at the turn of the century, that the lid finally blew off. The Yates books were looking more than a little suspicious and much was to come to the surface when Yates cheated Ford and Cooper, via their Argosy Productions company, by upping charges from 15 per cent to 35 per cent for facilities Yates was also using on other projects. However this was nothing to the creative accounting Yates was perpetrating on the box-office receipts from *The Quiet Man*. The contract drawn up had agreed a 50–50 split of net profits between Republic and Argosy. With word coming in from all around the country that the film was a smash-hit, the cash should have been flowing. But Yates's accounts were showing just half the anticipated amount. In Detroit and Chicago alone it had grossed $300,000 . . ..

Ford decided against a direct confrontation and went to a friend, the aptly-named 'Wild Bill' Donovan, a lawyer. Donovan, who had backed Ford's end of the *Quiet Man* project with finance, called in his own legal firm to begin an extensive and exhaustive audit on the Yates books. There were millions of dollars at stake and it stuck in Ford's throat that he had ended up doing his cherished project for what he called 'a back of the bus operation'. The problems then spilled over into personal relationships which led to rifts between Ford, Wayne and Cooper. Ford blamed Wayne for getting him involved with Yates although he forgave him a few months later. But he reckoned Cooper should have examined the small-print more carefully. A short time later, Cooper let it be known he'd had enough of Yates and quit working for Republic.

Chapter Eight
WHAT HAPPENED NEXT . . .

John Ford headed for East Africa to make *Mogambo* for Metro-Goldwyn-Mayer with Clark Gable and Grace Kelly and attempted to keep his mind off the financial wranglings with Herbert Yates back home.

While in Africa news came through that *The Quiet Man* had beaten off many big names and productions to win Ford his fourth Oscar as best director. Winton Hoch and Archie Stout both lifted Oscars for their magnificent Technicolor photography, and to complete a great night for the team, Merian Cooper received an Oscar for his many innovations and contributions to the art of motion pictures. With Ford on location, John Wayne collected the Oscar for his mentor when it could be argued that he should have been collecting one for himself.

Amid all the good news of awards, Ford heard that following the Donovan audit Yates wanted to make a cash settlement. At the same time the Republic chief made moves to put money into the Killanin-Ford project of Four Province Films in Ireland. Lord Killanin recalled: 'Jack's philosophy was that he preferred to be paid cash up front, rather than a percentage and all of the problems in hiring accountants to keep an eye on the profits. He didn't want to fight over money. His main interest was the finished article on the screen. There's no doubt that until it was released, Herbert Yates didn't know what he had got in terms of a great picture.'

The telegrams and cables began flying again:

25 March 1953 – Killanin to Ford: 'My dear Jack, It was certainly great news about your Oscar and everyone here sends their congratulations. Yates arrived safely on Sunday surrounded by mysterious henchmen. He is very enthusiastic and asked me to lunch on Monday. The only thing he said was that you should direct all four pictures.'

Ford cabled Killanin:

> Having acrimonious legal business complications with Monsieur de la Republic [Herb Yates]. Suing in process. Just won't pay his obligations. So stall, procrastinate and linger. Absolutely impossible for me personally to do business with him.

Maureen O'Hara, who had been approached by the new Four Province company, wrote from 662, Stone Canyon Road, West Los Angeles to Lord Killanin at the new film premises, 11 Wellington Quay, Dublin:

> Dear Michael, Yes, Jack did speak to me about the *Demi-gods* and I immediately read the book, which I had not had the pleasure of reading before. I know that it will make a wonderful picture. Of course in my opinion, when John Ford directs a picture, it is always great. It should not be difficult to turn the book into a screen play and I cannot wait to read your first treatment. I imagine you will await Jack's return from Africa before getting down to final plans and discussions. At that time we can then discuss my availability and all business matters.
>
> I am trying to arrange to be in Ireland within the next three months. Naturally I would like to be in Dublin but in any event I will let you know immediately I have definite plans. You know that I wish Four Province Films the greatest success in the world and, with Jack at the helm, there can be no failure. 'The Quiet Man' is doing wonderful business here and it gives us all a warm feeling to see an Irish picture so successful.
>
> Please give my best wishes and regards to Sheila and also to everyone at Spiddal. Sincerely Yours, Maureen.

30 July 1953 – Ford to Killanin:

> I saw a reel of 'The Quiet Man' on the big screen the other night and it was magnificent. Things that you didn't notice

133

on the small screen popped up. The bends on the river and the background were lovely and the characters seemed so much more vital. I look forward to seeing the entire film on the big screen when my eyes permit.

September brought sadness to all involved in *The Quiet Man* when Ford's brother, Francis, the old, white-bearded man in the film, became the first of the team to pass away. On 15 September Ford's personal assistant, known to all simply as Meta, wrote to Lord Killanin:

> Dear Michael, Himself is en route to the East primarily to pay the customary visit to his oldest brother in Maine, but you know more about the traditional Irish customs than I. Frank went very quietly in his sleep after a long, bad illness. Pappy and Wingate were with him and he roused a bit before the end and indicated he knew they were with him. The church was thronged with people for the Rosary and the Mass next morning and the shrinking number of old-timers was really pathetic – old actors and friends of many years' standing. Pappy was wonderful through it all but I know he feels the loss deeply. I'm glad he got away from here a bit.

John Ford wrote to Lord Killanin the same week:

> Dear Michael, your letter received and it was so good at this particular time to hear from Ireland, especially Spiddal. Frank had an easy passing and all his thoughts were about Ireland. His last hours all he could speak was Irish. The services were in the Irish tradition much to the horror of Joseph Ignatius O'Connor, the undertaker or 'mortician' as he prefers to be called . . . third generation Irish and looks it.
>
> Father James Thornton, Marteen's brother, helped officiate and he was carried to his grave by his brothers, sons and nephews in uniform. It was quite a galaxy including navy, marines, infantrymen, an air-force general and myself. Your telegram was most welcome to the immediate family, particularly to my sisters Mary and Josephine who were glad to hear

that the people in Spiddal had been informed. All in all I've
had a trying week.

With deep affection, Jack.

Ford wrote again on 28 September:

Dear Michael, I've just returned from a hurried trip to Maine to
see my oldest brother, Pat, and to report to him about Frank's
sickness and funeral. He was terribly touched about the news
that all the relatives in Galway had been duly notified and that
a Mass would be said. Our cousin, Bishop Feeney of Maine,
had a private Mass for members of the family there. I hope
to be in Europe soon and I sincerely hope that we can get
together. Please give all my love to the family and again my
thanks for your sympathy on Frank's death. We were terribly
pleased particularly about the Mass at Spiddal. As ever, Jack.

In October 1953 a memorable day was arranged for Ford when
the cast of *The Quiet Man* assembled at the Republic lot to pay
tribute to their director. John Wayne, Maureen O'Hara, Ward
Bond, Victor McLaglen, Charles FitzSimons and many of the
backroom team were there to salute and honour their boss. Maureen
O'Hara sang two songs from the movie, 'Wild Colonial Boy' and
'Galway Bay', while after dinner, prop man Ace Holmes wheeled
in a trolley holding the awards. George Sidney, President of the
Directors' Guild, presented Ford with the Guild's gold disc, Ward
Bond presented him with his Oscar and John Wayne acted as master
of ceremonies. Ford was visibly moved by such a turn-out and
this craggy Irish-American contradiction of a man was obviously
touched by the warmth of friends and colleagues on whom he
had sometimes been very hard, a fact referred to earlier by Lord
Killanin.

Ford was back in top form and he cabled Lord Killanin: 'Your
letter received with the discouraging news that the Reds – one John
Huston [his great director rival] – are seeking refuge in our lovely
Ireland. This aint good, he is not of the right wing.'

Another read: 'I've found out what an Episcopalian is. A Catholic
who has flunked his Latin! We received an Apostolic blessing from
his Holiness. Mary was made a Dame of the Order of San Salvador
and St Brigid.'

14 March 1955 – letter from Yates to Ford: 'You can rest assured that Republic lives up to all its contractural obligations.'

At last, in 1956, after three years of litigation, Yates finally paid Ford and Merian C. Cooper $546,000 each to cover three films – *Rio Grande*, released back in 1950, *The Quiet Man* and *The Sun Shines Bright*. It had been a long wait and not a pleasant experience for the Argosy Productions pair.

Chapter Nine
AND THEN . . .

Francis Ford had been the first of the *Quiet Man* team to pass away just two years after they had been on location in Ireland. In 1956 there was further sadness when the wonderful composer, Victor Young, died at the age of just 56. He had more than 300 movie scores to his credit although he worked with John Ford only three times, their first partnership coming in *Rio Grande* in 1950. After *The Quiet Man* he also scored *The Sun Shines Bright* for Ford. His first film had been *Fatal Lady* in 1936 and he won an Oscar in his very last movie, which was released the year after his death – *Around the World in 80 Days*. His work was wide ranging, from comedies such as *The Paleface* in 1948 to the classic western *Shane* in 1953. Sadly, Victor McLaglen also died, in 1959 at the age of 73. His final film, *Sea Fury*, had been released the previous year.

On 15 February 1960 John Ford cabled Lord Killanin: 'So I've got to help Duke with "The Alamo". This is a picture that actually costs five million dollars. It is a helluva picture, a real spectacular. But as I said, I have to help him.' This is the very opposite of an account given by John Wayne's third wife, Pilar, in her book *My Life with Duke*. She says Wayne told her that Ford turned up uninvited and Wayne let him shoot some second-unit scenes to preserve their life-long friendship, although these were left on the cutting-room floor. Wayne and Pilar had a daughter, Aissa, who appeared in what was the actor's tribute to Texas, a film he directed and in which he starred with Richard Widmark. Again there was a *Quiet Man* connection because in Aissa's birthday-party scene in the movie, Ken Curtis sings to his 'daughter' – the same Curtis who sang and played the accordion in Cohan's Bar as Dermot Fahy – 'no E squireen Danaher'. Curtis was one of The Sons of the Pioneers who sang in several Ford westerns and was, in fact, the director's son-in-law.

Although several of Wayne's associates died around this period, the sudden death of Ward Bond from a heart attack at the age of just 57, nine years after that glorious summer in Ireland, devastated Wayne and Ford. His untimely death came in Dallas, Texas, on 13 November 1960. Not surprisingly, he had gone to the Lone Star State to watch a football match. Aptly it had been that same sport which led to him meeting Wayne and becoming a movie star. He often featured as the rugged, kind-hearted lawman and was in Ford's *Drums Along the Mohawk* in 1939. He played Boots Mulcahy in *They Were Expendable* in 1945, Morgan Earp in *My Darling Clementine* in 1946, Sergeant Major O'Rourke in *Fort Apache* and Perley 'Buck' Sweet in *Three Godfathers* both in 1948, and then Elder Wiggs in *Wagonmaster* three years later, the movie on which television would base the popular series *Wagon Train* in the late fifties and give Bond the big starring role.

John Ford immediately shut down filming of *Two Rode Together*, starring James Stewart and Richard Widmark and involving a number of the *Quiet Man* team – screenwriter Frank S. Nugent, editor Jack Murray, assistant director Wingate Smith and actors Ken Curtis, Mae Marsh and Major Sam Harris. He flew to Los Angeles where he took over the funeral arrangements. The body was flown home from Dallas and taken to the Field Photographic Farm which Ford had set up at great personal expense to cater for the needs of veteran ex-movie men who had served in the forces. He posted a uniformed guard around the flag-draped coffin which stood in a chapel which had a Catholic crucifix, Protestant cross and the Star of David. Flags flew at half-mast and on the day of the funeral the coffin was placed on the parade ground and surrounded by wreaths from all over the country. John Wayne, choking with emotion and tears showing in his eyes, spoke the eulogy for his friend. The Sons of the Pioneers rendered 'The Song of the Wagonmaster'. Just before his death, and with his popularity at an all-time high with audiences, Bond had talked Ford and Wayne into doing a special episode of *Wagon Train* and Wayne broke his strict rule of not appearing in television productions as a gesture to his friend. The *Colter Craven Story*, a civil-war tale, featured a drunken doctor still affected by the horrors of the Battle of Shiloh who, just like Doc Holliday in *My Darling Clementine*, sobers up to perform a life-saving operation. Neither Ford nor Wayne could have imagined that by the time they watched the episode on their television screens their great friend would have gone. Looking back to when Bond had gatecrashed the movie *Salute* in 1929 when they had not got on so well, Wayne was to say: 'I remember telling him he was too damned ugly to be a movie star but I was wrong. He was beautiful where it counted – on the inside.'

Just a few months after Bond's funeral came news that the lovely Barry Fitzgerald had also passed away. He died in his beloved Dublin, after years in Hollywood, on 4 January 1961, just a couple of months short of his 73rd birthday. The little blue-eyed, red-haired Fitzgerald, just five-foot three, had remained very active and, until he retired back to his native Dublin in 1958, he could often be seen motor-cycling to and from the film studios. He appeared in more than 30 movies, working with John Wayne, Mildred Natwick, Ward Bond and his own brother, Arthur Shields, plus Victor McLaglen's brother Cyril, for the first time in John Ford's *The Long Voyage Home* in 1940; he played Cocky on board the *Glencairn* off a Caribbean island – a wartime movie. He worked with Maureen O'Hara for the first time in *How Green Was My Valley* and the only other time he worked with her was in *The Quiet Man*.

One of the screen's most delightful senior citizens, Barry Fitzgerald took ill and underwent brain surgery in Dublin in October 1959, just a year after retiring. When he passed away 15 months later his funeral was conducted from St Patrick's Cathedral on 9 January by The Most Reverend Dr Simms, Archbishop of Dublin. His first film had been *Juno and the Paycock* in 1930 and his last two were *Rooney* in 1957 and *Broth of a Boy* in 1959. In *The Quiet Man* he had classic lines, many of them to do with drink. His entrance to the movie at Castletown station brings a short, sharp: 'Innisfree? This way', which is followed by such familiar lines as: 'Ah nonsense man, it's only a mirage brought on by your terrible thirst – come up Napoleon'; 'When I drink whisky I drink whisky and when I drink water I drink water'; 'I don't suppose there's a drop of anything wet in the house'; and 'Buttermilk? The Borgias would do better.' Other great lines include: 'It's a bold, sinful man you are, Sean Thornton, and who taught you to be playing patty fingers in the holy water?'; 'Easy now, easy now, is this a courting or a Donnybrook? Have the good manners not to hit the man until he's your husband and entitled to hit you back'; and 'The Marquis of Queensberry Rules will be observed at all times, non-belligerents will kindly remain neutral.' His last line as he drives Red Will and the Widow Tillane in the horse and trap

May Craig and Barry Fitzgerald meet again in the late fifties

is: 'No patty-fingers please, the proprieties at all times. Hold on to your hats.'

1963 saw John Ford release *Donovan's Reef* which also marked his farewell to his yacht, the *Araner*. It held many memories for him, such as Ward Bond's marriage to Doris Sellers on board in 1935. Bond and John Wayne had been frequent visitors and it was, in fact, instrumental in Ford and Wayne being reunited after they had lost touch for a spell. By pure chance Wayne had been sitting in a quayside bar after one of his big fall-outs with first wife Josephine and discovered the *Araner* was moored just around the corner. From that point on, their professional relationship was to last uninterrupted for the rest of their lives. Wayne had gone on to become an overnight star thanks to Ford's movie *Stagecoach*, although the director, Howard Hawks, could also take enormous credit for launching Wayne to super-stardom through another western, *Red River*.

The Ford family had spent half their lives on the *Araner*, often sailing the Pacific from California to Hawaii as Ford prepared and studied scripts for filming, and the yacht had been used by the US Navy during the war. By the early sixties, however, its upkeep was threatening to become ruinous to him, so it was given its last hurrah when used in *Donovan's Reef* – a movie which used seven of the *Quiet Man* team, including Mae Marsh, who had been Father Paul's doting mother, and Major Sam Harris, another Ford favourite who had played the 'general', sitting aloofly in Cohan's Bar as the mayhem built around him. *Donovan's Reef*, like *The Quiet Man*, had a tremendous fight scene and some of the same shrew-taming tensions, with Wayne, as the chauvinistic Michael Patrick 'Guns' Donovan, proclaiming: 'From now on, I'll wear the pants.' Wayne and hell-raiser Lee Marvin played opposite Elizabeth Allen and Dorothy Lamour who, for once, had shaken off Hope and Crosby! Ford had sailed John Wayne and his children to the location and immediately after filming had been completed, the *Araner* was sold for a song.

The sixties saw Maurice Walsh still at work with his writing. He was not as prolific and his style was no longer as fashionable in a fast-changing world. However *The Quiet Man* was still very much in the news. On 8 and 9 August 1960, *The New York Times* reported that Fred Herbert was to produce a musical based on *The Quiet Man* called *Donnybrook*, with Jack Cole as choreographer and Eddie Foy as the star. It flopped and Maurice Walsh said in an interview: '*The Quiet Man* was first published in the *Saturday Evening Post* and later incorporated in *Green Rushes*. The scene was in my native Kerry. John Ford, who made the film, transferred the scene to Connemara and now Mr Herbert brings it up to Donnybrook. Fair enough!'

This was said with more than a hint of sarcasm and maybe even with a touch of exasperation as Donnybrook is an area in the south side of Dublin which was once the scene of a famous fair and is a word synonymous with the type of punch-up in the movie. There was obviously disappointment for Walsh in the musical's failure because he had enjoyed fresh adulation after the release of the film which he said he had enjoyed immensely. Following the première he declared: 'The picture is just good entertainment but the Technicolor of the Connemara scenes is extraordinarily fine. Moreover, Barry Fitzgerald steals the show.' Walsh was very much a Barry Fitzgerald fan and said that a character, Jamesy Coffey, in another of his works would have fitted the actor 'as a hand in a glove'. When *The Quiet Man* was released in 1952 Walsh's books were given a fresh boost. The movie is said to have grossed more at the box office in Paris than *Gone With the Wind*.

And it led to a new edition of Walsh's work – *L'Homme Tranquil*. In Germany it was *Der Stille Man* and Dutch, Danish and Swedish versions were also published. It was a similar situation in Canada, Australia and South Africa. Walsh, who very much approved of Maureen O'Hara for the female lead in the film, was awarded the American Screenwriters' Guild trophy, for originating the best-written comedy in America. It was only the fifth time the award had been presented and such was the clamour surrounding *The Quiet Man* after its release, that the story was dramatised in several forms including a version for the Listowel Writers' Week when it was performed in and around O'Sullivan's Bar at Ballydonoghue and at a pub in Listowel, now named 'The Quiet Man'. All of this was televised by RTE and delighted the inhabitants of Walsh's own local area. There had been attempts to sell the film rights of other Maurice Walsh works and the author himself had hoped that the Abbey Theatre in Dublin would put on his play *The Golden Pheasant* but it was rejected. His work was, however, heard on radio, including Scottish radio which dramatised *The Key Above the Door* over seven Sunday evenings.

The Quiet Man had not been the only time the paths of Walsh and Republic Pictures crossed, however. Following their joint success in 1952, negotiations had begun for *Trouble in the Glen*. Walsh's publishers, Chambers, sought £5,000 but Brandt and Brandt in America reckoned Walsh had accepted too small a fee for *The Quiet Man* and that he had been misled. The author then decided to go for £5,400 but Republic had dug in their heels and in the end paid out just under £4,000. Walsh hated this type of negotiation and the general atmosphere it created. *Trouble in the Glen* finally appeared in 1954 starring Margaret Lockwood and John Laurie. Walsh had been asked to assist during location work in Scotland but refused. He did not want to be any part of it and, in fact, didn't like the movie when he saw it.

This was really the end of his involvement in films concerning his own works, although in 1957 he got involved in a joint venture to write the screenplay for a film of Compton Mackenzie's *Whisky Galore*. Walsh, apart from having grown into a great writer, was also a man who generated great kindness and he was much loved and admired wherever he went. In Steve Matheson's *The Story-teller* he is described in later life as 'a small man with twinkling, sharp eyes, a golden tongue and a big heart'. He looked very distinguished with his white beard, tweed cloak, with its Wallace-tartan lining, and hat. He would encourage aspiring authors by saying: 'Look, if John Walsh's son from Ballydonoghue can do it so can you.' His home in Dublin, Green Rushes, was always a busy, warm house, full of friends, neighbours and laughter. Despite the Irish Catholicism which was bred into him – he twice turned his back on the Church and twice returned – like John Ford he seemed to revel in irreverence and would call himself a Communist and his dog Bolshie to shock anyone with narrow Catholic views. He was simply a Christian socialist who hated bigotry and hypocrisy in all their forms. Generally he remained a private man, giving just one television interview about his memories of Scotland, and he courteously refused an approach from Eamonn Andrews to appear on the TV show *What's My Line*. For his 79th birthday friends commissioned a bust of him in bronze. At 81 he was planning a visit to Edinburgh for the Festival although deteriorating health halted that ambition. He did, however, make a trip back to Kerry a year before his death and spent a day walking around the farm on his own, obviously realising it was a final farewell. It is not surprising that when he died in Dublin in 1964 at the age of 85 he was busy on the proofs of his final work, *The Smart Fellow*, which was published posthumously. President Eamonn de Valera attended the funeral Mass at St John the Baptist Church in Blackrock.

The great storyteller was buried, wearing his tweed cloak, in Esker Cemetery at Lucan, beside his wife, Caroline, who had died in 1940 at the age of 54 following a difficult birth, and their daughter, Elizabeth, who had died at just three months. The simple headstone reads: 'Maurice Walsh, Author. Born County Kerry 1879. Died Dublin 1964.' The main Walsh titles were: *And No Quarter*; *Blackcock's Feather*; *Green Rushes*; *The Hill is Mine*; *The Road to Nowhere*; *The Small Dark Man*; *Sons of the Swordmaker*; *Thomaseen James*; *While Rivers Run*; *Son of Apple*; *Castle Gillian*; *Trouble in the Glen*; *Son of a Tinker*; *The Honest Fisherman*; *A Strange Woman's Daughter*; *Danger Under the Moon* and *The Smart Fellow*. Without his genius and imagination all who have taken so much pleasure from *The Quiet Man* would be considerably the poorer.

Screenwriter Frank S. Nugent passed away in 1966 at the age of 58. He had worked with John Ford since *Fort Apache* in 1948 and *She Wore a Yellow Ribbon* the following year. His other works included Maurice Walsh's *Trouble in the Glen, The Searchers, The Last Hurrah* and *Donovan's Reef*. He worked on a total of ten films for Ford and was a master of his craft. For *Fort Apache* he travelled out to the ruins of Fort Bowie and to Apache Pass where there are still markers inscribed 'Killed by Apaches'.

By the late sixties John Wayne's popularity was showing no signs of diminishing. In 1968 a TV poll declared him to be television's most popular star although it was a medium where he appeared only in his old films rather than in a TV series. Many an American would have voted for Wayne as President but he had contented himself with several White House visits during the years of the Roosevelt, Trueman, Eisenhower and Johnston administrations. Unlike John Ford, he was not a John F. Kennedy fan and did not visit during that presidency. When Richard Nixon took over from Johnston he sent Air Force One to pick up Wayne, his friends Bob Hope and James Stewart and their wives for a White House reception.

The following year, 1969, brought Wayne his finest hour when, after four decades of movie-making, he at last won an Oscar, beating off such strong competition as Peter O'Toole in *The Lion in Winter*, Richard Burton in *Anne of a Thousand Days* and Jon Voight in *Midnight Cowboy*. All had been nominated, but it was Wayne who triumphed, with his first nomination since *The Sands of Iwo Jima* in 1949. Admittedly there had been some unmemorable performances over the years but it was amazing that, having failed even to be nominated for *Stagecoach*, *Red River*, *She Wore a Yellow Ribbon*, *The Quiet Man* or *The Searchers*, it should be as an aging cowboy in *True Grit* that he would scoop his much-deserved award. At the age of 61 he was still doing many of his own stunts, despite being overweight and having just one good lung because of the ravages of cancer.

Wayne's address to the Academy as he clutched the statuette was delivered in a voice breaking with emotion:

> Ladies and gentlemen, I'm no stranger to this podium. I've come here and picked up these beautiful golden men before, but always for a friend. One night I picked up two, one for Admiral John Ford and one for our beloved Gary Cooper. I was very clever and witty that night, the envy of Bob Hope. But tonight I don't feel very clever, very witty. I feel very grateful, very humble, and I owe thanks to many, many people. I want to thank the members of the Academy. To all you people who are watching on television, thank you for taking such a warm interest in our glorious industry. Oscar and I have something in common. Oscar first came to Hollywood in 1928. So did I. We're both a little weather-beaten, but we're here and plan to be around for a whole lot longer.

Just over 12 months later, in 1970, John Wayne and Maureen O'Hara were reunited on the screen for the last time in *Big Jake* which saw the screen début of his son from his third marriage, Ethan. The year 1970 also saw the passing away of Arthur Shields, nine years after the death of his brother, Barry Fitzgerald. His films had ranged from *The Plough and the Stars* in 1937 to *The Pigeon that Took Rome* in 1962.

In 1973 no fewer than three of the *Quiet Man* team died. After quitting Argosy and at last getting his money from Herbert Yates in 1956, Merian C. Cooper had turned his back on Hollywood where he had pioneered the first use of colour in movies and the first musical-dancing motion picture and enjoyed 17 years of retirement. He had bought a small house in Coronado, California, built, aptly, in a military retirement community across the bay from San Diego, and he spent those years among army generals and admirals who had been friends since schooldays. He was author of two books and a founder of Pan Am and Western Airlines. His movies ranged from *Grass* in 1925 to *The Searchers* in 1956. This remarkable man died at the age of 83.

There was also great sadness at the death of Jack McGowran shortly after he had completed work on *The Exorcist*. Maureen O'Hara's stand-in, Etta Vaughan recalled:

> Jack was always in great form. I remember when Francis Ford came out the door of the house in the little side street of Cong waving his stick in the air as the fight started and Jack, who was watching, said to me: 'Did he shout "Up the IRA"?' He was always quick with a line and kept everyone going. He was a comedian in the real sense and very funny in real life. It said much for him that he could stay so humorous because he was quite ill during the making of *The Quiet Man*. He had something wrong with his liver and had to have liver injections every second day. He was perfect for the part of Feeney with that funny, sharp little head of his. He was comical, really comical and so spontaneous. His fun and his jokes made him a delightful character among those lovely Abbey Theatre people.

That same year saw John Wayne lose his 'movie father' when John Ford passed away on 31 August 1973 at his retirement home in Palm Desert. Just before the end he had been awarded the Presidential Medal of Freedom, America's highest civilian honour, for leaving his 'personal stamp indelibly printed on the consciousness of whole generations both here and abroad'. He was laid to rest beside his brother, Francis, although some friends felt he should have been buried in Monument Valley where he shot so many of his spectacular westerns. His coffin was covered by the American flag, which he had filmed being raised at Midway during the war, the battle in which he had been wounded. John Ford shot 134 films, *The Quiet Man* being the 108th and his most sentimental. His American background was always woven inextricably with the wild and lonesome beauty of Connemara.

From 1976 onwards Wayne himself was in poor health and he had struggled against pain to make his last film, *The Shootist*. By

Behind him all the way. When John Wayne had to get his feet wet in the courting scene, the Ford clan was there (left to right): John Ford, his son Patrick and brother Eddie O'Ferra

the late seventies it was obvious his time was running out, but not before he had been awarded perhaps his greatest honour. On 23 May 1979 the US Congress conducted hearings to vote on the minting of a special medal honouring Wayne. The bill had been introduced by his great friend in politics, Senator Barry Goldwater, who had run against Lyndon Johnston in the 1964 elections. Maureen O'Hara and Elizabeth Taylor testified before the Congress, while movie friends such as Frank Sinatra, Jack Lemmon, Katherine Hepburn, Gregory Peck, Kirk Douglas and James Stewart sent telegrams of support. The bill was passed unanimously and Wayne became only the 85th American to be honoured by the government in such a way. Others, since the medal's inception in 1776, had included George Washington, John Paul Jones, the Wright Brothers, Thomas Edison, Charles Lindbergh, Irving Berlin, Bob Hope and Robert Kennedy. The Congressional gold medal portrayed him in his *Alamo* role as Davy

Crockett on one side with Monument Valley on the other and the simple inscription, proposed by Maureen O'Hara: 'John Wayne, American.' It was apt for a man who had been the very apotheosis of the American male, the frontiersman and representative of the American dream. In 1971 he had been named by the Marine Corps League as 'the man who best exemplifies the word American'.

John Wayne hadn't gone to church throughout his life but he strongly believed in God without believing in organised religion. Towards the end of his fight against cancer at his home in Bayshore Drive, Newport Beach, California, Maureen O'Hara flew from St Croix to spend one last day with him. Typically she stayed for three, with his maid laundering her clothes day by day. Wayne's first wife, Josephine, had been Catholic and his four children from that marriage had been brought up in her faith. On his death-bed he converted to Catholicism before passing away on 11 June 1979 at 5.23 p.m. Pacific daylight time, his death making headlines all around the world. His last will and testament, signed Marion Morrison, ran to 27 pages, and he left $6.8 million, mostly property, to his children. It had been apt that his last movie, *The Shootist*, co-starring his lifelong friend James Stewart, had a story with which Wayne could identify – that of an ageing gunfighter dying of cancer.

Chapter Ten
MEMORIES ARE MADE OF THIS

Maureen O'Hara, her two brothers, Charles FitzSimons and James Lilburn, Mildred Natwick and Sean McClory are the only survivors now from that marvellous, unforgettable cast of 40 years ago and they still enjoy the most wonderful memories from the summer of 1951.

Maureen was always the classy colleen who was considered one of the cinema's true beauties. Photographers and movie cameramen said they could 'shoot' her from any angle and not be able to come up with a bad shot. One critic said: 'She looks as though butter would not melt in her mouth – or anywhere else' and another said: 'Framed in Technicolor, Miss O'Hara somehow seems more significant than a setting sun.' She was also dubbed 'spirited', 'decorative' and 'ornamental'. The critics hardly did her justice as, during the forties, she was always in the public's list of the five most beautiful women, thanks to her high cheekbones and attractively freckled, pale skin. Allied to all of this was a deep crimson blush which completed the perfect Technicolor complexion.

Her rebellious streak of Irish temperament and sudden anger could swiftly recede into a glowing Gaelic warmth and this made her ideally suited for *The Quiet Man*. She was a unique, unconventional screen heroine, aggressive and self-willed. One moment she would appear vulnerable and the next a veritable wildcat who cracked Tyrone Power on the head with a rock, out-fenced Errol Flynn, with eyes, teeth and rapier all flashing, and threw a few punches at John Wayne. She was directed by John Ford, Lewis Milestone, Jean Renoir, Alfred Hitchcock,

Sir Carol Reed, William Dieterle, William Wellman, Delmer Daves, Henry Hathaway and Henry King. She co-starred with John Wayne, James Stewart, Tyrone Power, Charles Laughton, Henry Fonda, Sir Alec Guinness, Dana Andrews, John Garfield, Ray Milland, Rex Harrison and Joel McCrea. Among her roles were Louis Cody, Buffalo Bill's wife, Spanish nobility, an Arabian princess, a college dean, a French gipsy, an English farmer, a bullfighter's lady, a swordswoman and western wildcat. In the business she was regarded as a good sport because she did many of her own stunts. She said of those adventure movies: 'I loved making those pictures and I think people liked looking at them. I loved the yashmaks and the camel films. In fact, to keep my feet on the ground, my family would call me Maureen Sahara!' And she added: 'Men don't know how to swashbuckle now. They don't know how to take off their plumed hats or make their eyes twinkle. It's the twinkle I miss most!'

Morale is sky-high among the extras and stars: (left to right) John Wayne, Maureen O'Hara, May Craig, Eric Gorman, Paddy O'Donnell and Webb Overlander

But despite her beauty and popularity some would say she never attained super-stardom, probably because she did not develop one special forte. She played heavy dramatics, high comedy, respectable classics, gentle romance, war films and epic westerns. But it was in John Wayne, particularly in *The Quiet Man*, that she found her perfect foil.

It was not long after filming *The Quiet Man* that Maureen and her second husband, Will Price, were divorced. After making her last movie with John Ford in 1957, *The Wings of Eagles*, she took out a $357,000 lawsuit against the magazine *Confidential* which put the publication out of business. It had made allegations about the personal lives of several Hollywood stars including hers. But she was the only one who had the courage to go to court and testify, which won her enormous respect.

In 1959, at the age of 39 she made *Our Man in Havana*, based on Graham Greene's novel, and the following year she made *The Parent Trap* with young Haley Mills and it grossed $11.3 million in the US alone. She then starred in *Mr Hobbs Takes a Vacation* with James Stewart and in *Spencer's Mountain* with Henry Fonda in 1963. That same year she was voted Actress of the Year by the Club Women of America who said her work was 'consistently upgrading and wholesome and far removed from the salacious themes which contaminate the minds and morals of American youth'. She commanded great respect off-screen too as, over the years, she had developed a reputation as a caring person and anything but a prima donna. This was echoed in recent years when she was given an Honorary Doctorate of Law at Galway University; during the ceremony it was said: 'She portrayed a beautiful, determined young woman with a fiery temperament who has created among young cinema audiences everywhere a unique, popular image of Ireland and its womanhood.' She was also the first recipient of the City of Cork Award presented at the Cork Opera House 'in recognition of her lasting contribution to the cinema'. Allan 'Whitey' Snyder, a behind-the-scenes Hollywood legend who had been Marilyn Monroe's make-up man and confidant described Miss O'Hara as a 'star' and a professional who never let success go to her head. John Wayne said he loved her ability to 'ride with the scene' if he suddenly broke from the script with an action or an ad lib. 'She was always quick enough to grasp the change and you just could not rattle her,' he said. She always had the determination, strength and ability to control a scene without sacrificing her femininity – even when clashing swords with Flynn or sharing fisticuffs with Wayne. She was looked upon as the perfect leading lady and a director's dream. She was never late which pleased the so-punctual Wayne. In *Big Jake* there had been a problem in completing her wardrobe on time and she suggested that some costumes from her previous films could be cleaned up and adapted, something few, if any other stars, would have accepted, never mind suggested. There is no doubt, she was John Ford's favourite and as close to him as his own children. Perhaps it was their mutual Irishness which drew them together. Lord Killanin recalled: 'I knew Maureen's family, as Jack Ford did, even before *The Quiet Man*. Her mother ran a ladies' dress shop in Dublin's Kildare Street and her father, Charlie FitzSimons, was the manager of Woodrow's hat shop. They emigrated to America when Maureen took them over there.'

Ford was obviously a good judge of an actress, being the most honoured American film director of all time. When she was working for someone else he would phone the location to check on his 'red-head' and she showed a wonderful devotion in return when he was seriously ill. Despite being on location in the backwater of Durango, Mexico, she would phone to his hospital bedside in Los Angeles every day no matter what the difficulty of getting a line. It was typical of the woman who had typed *The Quiet Man* script for him.

Big Jake, with John Wayne, had been her last feature film and was released exactly 20 years after the summer of 1951. Her only appearance after that was in a TV production entitled *The Red Pony* a year later. She had at last found true love and happiness on the island of St Croix in the US Virgin Islands with third husband Captain Charles Blair whom she worshipped. He was a great flier who had taken the first and last sea planes from the States to Foynes Harbour in Limerick and was the first to fly a commercial jet from Shannon Airport to the States. Tragically, while she spent a holiday in the west of Ireland in 1978, Maureen received news that his plane had crashed in St Croix and he had been killed. John Wayne, who had been their guest on the island the previous year, had been too ill by this time to attend the funeral but had got his political ally Barry Goldwater to arrange that Captain Blair be buried with full honours at Arlington National Cemetery in Washington DC. After his death, Maureen ran his flying company and was appointed President of Antilles Airboats Incorporated, based at the west sea-plane ramp on the island. She continued to run the company until 1989, in between constant visits to her other home at Glengariff in West Cork.

Despite her many years in Hollywood and St Croix, her heart remains very much in her native country. In an interesting letter to Lord Killanin in 1989 she wrote that we might not have heard the last of *The Quiet Man* or Mary Kate. 'I have been avoiding a number of projects in relation to "The Quiet Man" because of a discussion I have had in Hollywood about an authorised possible sequel to the story-line which is enormously tempting financially.' Her brother Charles has a sequel script in which the Quiet Man's son follows in his father's footsteps, emigrates to America, becomes a prize fighter and is matched against the son of the boxer killed in the ring by his father in the original movie. But just like John Ford, Charles FitzSimons is finding more than a little difficulty in raising the cash to start production. 'It's a great script,' he said at his Los Angeles home. 'It's packed with action and I reckon it will do well. It is set against the ethnic background of the Irish-Americans and Italian-Americans in the US.' It is thanks to *The Quiet Man* that Charles now lives in America and has done so well in the movie industry. But life was not always kind – especially when he was a young, struggling actor. He recalled:

I took part in a play at the Citizen's Theatre in Glasgow in the forties, and I remember staying at the old Adelphi Hotel. The waiter eyed me rather suspiciously for a while but then exclaimed: 'You're no' English, you're Irish. You'll have a steak.' He pulled a screen around my table and served me a magnificent steak at a time when you would have killed for a decent piece of meat. I hadn't eaten anything worthwhile in weeks. I was involved in another play in London which flopped and I had neither my rent nor the fare back to Ireland. It was then that I met John Ford's unit production manager, Lee Lukather. He had been told I was an Irish Barrister-At-Law with intimate knowledge of the theatre in London and Ireland. I travelled to Ireland with him to help set up locations and introduce him to contacts. I organised the use of the train for the opening scene, through the Irish government, and we toured all the areas to be used. It was the bitter winter of 1950 and we thought we were going to freeze to death.

It was bad enough for a native like me but this poor Yank must have thought he'd landed on the moon. I remember we would go back to Ashford Castle in the evenings and stand in front of heaters trying to thaw out. Lee died a few years ago which was very sad for all of us. He was a wonderful man, very determined and the best in the business as a Hollywood unit manager. During filming he was trying to hustle an Irish worker who had a load of lumber on his shoulder. As Lee tried to speed things up the man slowly removed his load, placed it on the ground and said: 'The man who made time made plenty of it.' This, of course, was something Hollywood viewed with horror. Time was money. The worker then picked up his load and continued at his own pace. Thereafter Lee was known as 'Mr Lucifer'!

Like most of the cast, Charles got on well with John Ford who was godfather to one of his children. But like most, he also had his disagreements with him. He recalled:

The day we were shooting the train coming into Castletown I suggested we have the camera up on the railway bridge because you could see a good two miles from there. But he said to me: 'Charlie, when you talk to someone do you lie on the floor and look up at them, do you climb a ladder and look down at them or do you look them in the eye?' 'Look them in the eye,' I replied. 'Well, that's the way I make movies and the camera will be on the platform watching the train come in.' Outside the church for the holy water scene with Maureen and Duke I had made a suggestion about the best time for the light and he said sarcastically: 'In Ireland does the sun rise in the east and set in the west?'

However, he did listen to me for one important scene. He was threatening at one stage to cut that lovely scene of Maureen and Duke in the rose garden behind the White O' Mornin' cottage because he thought Duke's fans would not want to see him in such a gentle romantic mood picking a small flower and handing it to his new wife. I loved the scene and pleaded with him to leave it in which thankfully he did.

John Ford and Merian C. Cooper were, of course, a terrific team but John would make changes which sometimes left you wondering. If, for instance, you watch closely during the wedding-reception scene you will see my lips pronounce a word which was edited out. When I toasted the couple my line was: 'May they live in peace and national freedom.' But John Ford panicked a bit thinking the word 'national' might offend and it leads to a slight break in the sound. There was supposed to be a greater IRA – Black-and-Tans theme but he changed it.

We all had so many happy times in Ireland and I remember the very first scene I watched being shot was at Yeates Castle about 20 miles from Cong. Maureen took off her shoes and stockings to run across the stream in the courting scene and as she ran out of shot I caught her in my arms. I did the same when she ran across the other stream at the White O' Mornin' cottage. When you see the water being whipped up by the wind, that was genuine. There were no machines involved and it looks very dramatic.

John Ford enjoyed a joke and he had a great sense of humour. I remember him roaring one day when Kevin Lawless's father was driving us about. Puffing his umpteenth cigarette of the day, Lawless senior pointed into a cemetery and said: 'See that, it's full of people who gave up smoking.'

The memories are quite wonderful and I have a constant reminder of the film in that I kept my jacket from it. Maureen has the original jaunting trap from the film at her home in Cork.

Charles recalled his first meeting with Mildred Natwick too:

> I was walking through Ashford Castle when I heard this lady shouting 'Let me out!' She thought she had locked herself in a toilet but in fact was pulling at the door when, for reasons best known to the builders, it had to be pushed outwards on to a corridor. That was another of the many laughs and we became good friends.

Mildred Natwick, one of the American Theatre's most expert comediennes, could also play the straight-faced, straight-laced parts and she was well suited to play the Widow Tillane. A real character actress, she was at her best in eccentric roles. The *Long Voyage Home* in 1940 had been the first of four films in which she was directed by Ford, a film based on Eugene O'Neill's play. The others were *Three Godfathers* in 1948, and *She Wore a Yellow Ribbon* a year later. Then came *The Quiet Man*. It was a source of great joy while researching this story to discover she was alive and well at the age of 82 and living at one of New York's most prestigious addresses in magnificent Park Avenue, just along from the world's most famous hotel, the Waldorf Astoria. Living up to the reputation bestowed upon her by the people of Cong all those years earlier as a kind, considerate person, Miss Natwick replied to my inquiries and said in subsequent interviews:

> My memories of my only visit to Ireland are a bit faded now although I do remember the charm, the warmth and the reality of those adorable people in the village.
>
> It is lovely to know all these years on that I am remembered by the likes of Mary Gibbons and the O'Connors. The O'Connors' little daughter of whom I was so fond is well grown up now and I've heard lives here in the States, in Virginia, so maybe we can get together again. It was a happy trip and as nice a time as I enjoyed during my career. I loved Ashford Castle and made great friends of Eileen Crowe and Barry Fitzgerald. How we all miss Barry.
>
> I remember when we arrived in Cong they were still a few weeks away from having electricity. The other memory is that everyone seemed to go about on bicycles. It was John Ford who gave the signal for the big switch-on just before we all returned to the States and I have a vivid recollection of there being three lamps to light the main street.
>
> Lord Killanin was very kind and helped me put on an English accent for my part. He spent a fair bit of time coaching me because I sounded very American. It was because of his efforts that I got it just right for the part. Another memory I have is of passing the old stone cross of Cong in the middle of the street just outside Cohan's the day we all went off to the beach for the horse-race scenes.

Joker Barry Fitzgerald dons a railway hat, much to the amusement of (left to right) Eric Gorman, Eileen Crowe, Joseph O'Dea and May Craig

Miss Natwick said of her background: 'I was born in Baltimore, Maryland.' And, shrilling as she did in the movie when rebuking Sean Thornton for wishing to turn White O' Mornin' 'into a national shrine', saying that 'my own family, Mr Thornton, has been in Ireland since the Normans came some hundreds of years ago', she revealed, with some pride, her family tree in real life. 'My mother's family were from England and my father's from Norway.' She added:

> I loved working with John Ford and John Wayne. Strangely, I have never met up with Maureen O'Hara since *The Quiet Man*. Our paths have never crossed. I still watch the movie and they have it on television here every St Patrick's Day.
>
> I've had a wonderful career including Broadway appearances but I think it is safe to say now that I have retired. I flew to France and stayed in Paris in 1988 for my last movie – *Dangerous Liaisons* – with Glenn Close and John Malkovich which was made by Warner Brothers and Lorimar. Now I'm

quite happy to spend my time seeing my friends for lunch and going to the theatre.

It's amazing how *The Quiet Man* has kept its popularity and that new generations watch it in great numbers. I just wish John Ford was still around today to enjoy the acclaim.

I'm sure he would love to know.

CONCLUSION

Why was, and indeed why is, *The Quiet Man* such a popular film? In earlier pages Lord Killanin described it as 'a western made in Ireland' by John Ford's travelling stock company of actors and actresses who appeared in so many of his movies. Charles FitzSimons, in a recent conversation from his Los Angeles home, called it 'a fairytale version of Ireland shot in a quaint village just off Sunset Boulevard'.

Is it down to Maurice Walsh's lovely, original story? Or is it because of Ford's treatment of the story line? Is it because of the special chemistry created by John Wayne, Maureen O'Hara and a splendid supporting cast in the shape of a village full of congenital busybodies? Or has the breathtaking Irish landscape much to do with the movie's success? The secret, I suspect, is a little bit of everything fusing into a winning combination.

The charming, quirky, eccentric characters create rumbustious humour, passionate romance and slapstick farce, and it is easy to forget that just under the surface lies unhappiness, hurt and guilt. Mary Kate Danaher, like Katherina in *The Taming of the Shrew*, is wilful, elicits sympathy and succeeds in bringing the war of the sexes to an honourable settlement. Of course Katherina is married against her will to the fortunehunter, Petruchio – although later actresses have softened the role to indicate she does, in fact, fall in love with him at first sight. Like the famous Shakespeare play, *The Quiet Man* too has its separate 'frame' in which a hoax is perpetrated – here, between Red Will Danaher and the Widow Tillane – and has a plot cleverly interwoven with folklore and classic comedy. Wife-taming stories abounded in classical, medieval and renaissance literature and most had the same ending. Katherina became an obedient wife. So to did Mary Kate. 'I'll have the supper ready for you.'

Walsh's story was a serious piece based on Ireland in the twenties, a time of armed resistance, foreboding and fright, an insecure country dominated by an insular church. Oil lamps and candles dimly lit the lives of a nation of which 90 per cent lived in abject poverty with only the doctors, some clerics and the more successful merchants well off. At least it is fair to say everyone else there was in the same boat. It was a repressed society with everybody quite sure they were going to hell.

From such a stark reality, Ford, whose Irishness was implicit in so much of his work, managed to fashion not just romantic wistfulness but in fact turned *The Quiet Man* into a story and film of uncomplicated amusement through his inventiveness and ability to adapt and change, even as the cameras rolled. From the claustrophobic press of church and home in that era he created a carousel of fieldwork, harvests and weddings while mixing in all the emotional themes of family love and hatred, ritual futility and moral hypocrisy.

Maybe the director was helped by the fact that even by 1951 parts of rural Ireland were still essentially 19th-century communities with horses and carts on the roads, people cutting their own turf for fuel and still anything but well off despite much of the appalling poverty subsiding. Even in some parts of Ireland today people toil long and hard cutting turf in the bogs and it is still a nation called twice a day to prayer – at noon and at six p.m. – as the Angelus bell sounds not only above churches but on national radio and television. So there are still traces of *The Quiet Man* atmosphere in many parts of the country.

The movie allowed Ford to indulge in a studied sensuality lacking in his other films. There are sexual innuendos with lines like: 'I can think of a few things I'd like to do to one of the Danahers, Miss Danaher' . . . 'Good morning, yes, but it was good night you had on your mind' . . . 'A man would have to be a sprinter to catch his wife in a bed like that', plus, of course, the broken bed scene itself and Michaeleen's reaction of 'Impetuous'. But Ford never stepped beyond the boundaries of good taste, a taste shared by his stars. Maureen O'Hara once said: 'Apart from

Conclusion

John Ford (seated) while Wayne, O'Hara and Fitzgerald wait on the pony trap at the beginning of the courting scene

the sinful amounts of money people are paid today, money which only goes to the taxman when it could be used to make better films, I don't approve of the explicit scenes. After all, the greatest love stories in the world were made without that and something was left to the imagination of the people. Everyone thinks in a different way about what means an awful lot to them in love, kindness and warmth. So let each person have their own dream. Why make it so explicit on the screen in such an ugly way.' John Wayne, in the very last interview he gave, on a Barbara Walters TV special broadcast on 13 March 1979, just weeks before his death, admitted 'Women scare the hell out of me.' And the thrice-married actor added: 'I've always been afraid of them.' Then, recalling those memorable days in Ireland 28 years earlier, he said: 'I wasn't a sex symbol but I enjoyed *The Quiet Man*, the relationship with Maureen O'Hara, because it was healthy, strong and sensual but it was not degrading.' And Maurice Walsh drew this tribute from Douglas Newton in a publication of the time, *G.K.'s Weekly*:

Maurice Walsh will charm his hundreds of thousands of readers anew with *Green Rushes*. I confess I am one of his most ready victims. Any man who writes so graciously, who can move the spirit with that clear glow of loveliness which seems but the sunset's aftermath in a world given over to the True and the Unbeautiful, must demand affection. He is an accomplished artist; he disdains dirt; he turns to the old spiritual fundamentals of courage and honour, charity, sweetness and human dignity; he quarries among the simple and common activities of life for his themes, finding a hundred things to write about where others only find sex. He is never 'clever' or 'brilliant'. Yet his readers are a thousand to most others' one. He is, of course, the genius turned story-teller. In his own field, Maurice Walsh has no superior.

Walsh was reputed to have sold around 400,000 books by the mid-thirties and the *Manchester City News* commented on *Green Rushes*: 'There are passages of startling poetic beauty; there are others of sentiment sweet beyond forgiveness. Of the author's technical mastery there is never a moment's doubt. The story's pattern is superb.'

The Quiet Man is a story for all ages and all age groups. Children today are as enthralled by the movie as their parents and grandparents were and it promises to bring joy and entertainment for generations to come. Walsh's characters were always gloriously alive on the page. John Ford found the right actors, injected both Homer and humour, and the rest is cinematic history.

THE FILMS

JOHN FORD: *The Tornado, The Scrapper, The Soul Herder, Cheyenne's Pal, Straight Shooting, The Secret Man, A Marked Man, Bucking Broadway* (1917); *The Phantom Riders, Wild Women, Thieves' Gold, The Scarlet Drop, Hell Bent, A Woman's Fool, Three Mounted Men* (1918); *Roped, The Fighting Brothers, A Fight for Love, By Indian Post, The Rustlers, Bare Fists, Gun Law, The Gun Packer, Riders of Vengeance, The Last Outlaw, The Outcasts of Poker Flat, The Ace of the Saddle, The Rider of the Law, A Gun Fightin' Gentleman, Marked Men* (1919); *The Prince of Avenue A, The Girl in Number 29, Hitchin' Posts, Just Pals, The Big Punch* (1920); *The Freeze Out, Desperate Trails, Action, Sure Fire, Jackie* (1921); *The Wallop, Little Miss Smiles, The Village Blacksmith* (1922); *The Face on the Barroom Floor, Three Jumps Ahead, Cameo Kirby, North of Hudson Bay, Hoodman Blind* (1923); *The Iron Horse, Hearts of Oak* (1924); *Lightnin', Kentucky Pride, The Fighting Heart, Thank You* (1925); *The Shamrock Handicap, Three Bad Men, The Blue Eagle* (1926); *Upstream* (1927); *Mother Machree, Four Sons, Hangman's House, Napoleon's Barber, Riley the Cop* (1928); *Strong Boy, The Black Watch, Salute* (1929); *Men Without Women, Born Reckless, Up the River* (1930); *Seas Beneath, The Brat, Arrowsmith* (1931); *Air Mail, Flesh* (1932); *Pilgrimage, Dr Bull* (1933); *The Lost Patrol, The World Moves On, Judge Priest* (1934); *The Whole Town's Talking, The Informer, Steamboat Round the Bend* (1935); *The Prisoner of Shark Island, Mary of Scotland, The Plough and the Stars* (1936); *Wee Willie Winkie, The Hurricane* (1937); *Four Men and a Prayer, Submarine Patrol* (1938); *Stagecoach, Young Mr Lincoln, Drums Along the Mohawk* (1939); *The Grapes of Wrath, The Long Voyage Home* (1940); *Tobacco Road* (1941); *Sex Hygiene, How Green Was My Valley* (1941); *The Battle of Midway, Torpedo Squadron* (1942); *December 7th, We Sail at Midnight* (1943); *They Were Expendable* (1945); *My Darling Clementine* (1946); *The Fugitive (1947); Fort Apache, Three Godfathers* (1948); *She Wore a Yellow Ribbon* (1949); *When Willie Comes Marching Home, Wagonmaster,*

163

Rio Grande (1950); *This Is Korea* (1951); *What Price Glory, The Quiet Man* (1952); *The Sun Shines Bright, Mogambo* (1953); *The Long Gray Line, Mister, Roberts, Rookie of the Year, The Bamboo Cross* (1955); *The Searchers* (1956); *The Wings of Eagles, The Rising of the Moon* (1957); *So Alone, The Last Hurrah* (1958); *Gideon of Scotland Yard, Korea, The Horse Soldiers* (1959); *The Colter Craven Story, Sergeant Rutlege* (1960); *Two Rode Together* (1961); *The Man Who Shot Liberty Vallance, Flashing Spikes, How The West Was Won* (1962); *Donovan's Reef* (1963); *Cheyenne Autumn* (1964); *Young Cassidy* (1965); *Seven Women* (1966); *Chesty: A Tribute to a Legend,* (1970); *Vietnam! Vietnam!* (1971)

JOHN WAYNE: *Mother Machree, Hangman's House* (1928); *Salute* (1929); *Men Without Women, Rough Romance, Cheer Up and Smile, The Big Trail* (1930); *Girls Demand Excitement, Three Girls Lost, Men Like That, Range Feud, Hurricane Express* (1931); *Shadow of the Eagle, Maker of Men, Two Fisted Law, Texas Cyclone, Lady and Gent, Ride Him Cowboy, The Big Stampede* (1932); *The Three Mesquiteers, Haunted Gold, Telegraph Trail, His Private Secretary, Central Airport, Baby Face Harrington, The Sagebrush Trail, Somewhere in Sonora, The Life of Jimmy Dolan, Baby Face,*

John Wayne between takes, outside the Danaher house

The Films

The Man From Monterey, Riders of Destiny, College Coach (1933); *West of the Divide, Blue Steel, Lucky Texan, The Man from Utah, Randy Rides Alone, Star Packer, The Trail Beyond, Neath Arizona Skies* (1934); *Texas Terror, The Lawless Frontier, New Frontier, Lawless Range, Rainbow Valley, Paradise Canyon, The Dawn Rider, Westward Ho, Desert Trail* (1935); *The Lawless Nineties, King of the Pecos, The Oregon Trail, Winds of the Wasteland, The Sea Spoilers, The Lonely Trail, Conflict* (1936); *California Straight Ahead, Cover the War, Idol of the Crowds, Adventure's End, Born to the West, Pals of the Saddle* (1937); *Overland Stage Raiders, Santa Fe Stampede, Red River Range* (1938); *Stagecoach, Night Riders, Three Texas Steers, Wyoming Outlaw, New Frontier, Allegheny Uprising* (1939); *Dark Command, Three Faces West, The Long Voyage Home, Seven Sinners, A Man Betrayed* (1940); *The Lady from Louisiana, The Shepherd of the Hills, Lady for a Night* (1941); *Reap the Wild Wind, The Spoilers, In Old California, Flying Tigers, Reunion in France, Pittsburg* (1942); *A Lady takes a Chance, In Old Oklahoma* (1943); *The Fighting Seabees, Tall in the Saddle, Back to Bataan, Flame of the Barbary Coast* (1944); *Dakota, They Were Expendable* (1945); *Without Reservations* (1946); *Angel and the Badman, Tycoon* (1947); *Fort Apache, Red River, Three Godfathers, Wake of the Red Witch* (1948); *The Fighting Kentuckian, She Wore a Yellow Ribbon, Sands of Iwo Jima* (1949); *Rio Grande* (1950); *Operation Pacific, Flying Lethernecks* (1951); *Big Jim McLain, The Quiet Man* (1952); *Trouble Along the Way, Island in the Sky, Hondo* (1953); *The High and the Mighty* (1954); *The Sea Chase, Blood Alley, The Conqueror, I Married a Woman* (1955); *The Searchers* (1956); *The Wings of Eagles, Jet Pilot* (1957); *The Barbarian and the Geisha* (1958); *Rio Bravo, The Horse Soldiers* (1959); *North to Alaska, The Alamo* (1960); *The Comancheros* (1961); *The Man Who Shot Liberty Vallance, Hatari, The Longest Day* (1962); *How the West Was Won, Donovan's Reef, McLintock* (1963); *Circus World* (1964); *The Greatest Story Ever Told, In Harm's Way, The Sons of Katie Elder* (1965); *Cast a Giant Shadow* (1966); *El Dorado, The War Wagon* (1967); *The Green Berets, Hellfighters* (1968); *The Undefeated, True Grit* (1969); *Rio Lobo, Chisum* (1970); *Big Jake* (1971); *The Cowboys* (1972); *The Train Robbers, Cahill* (1973); *McQ* (1974); *Brannigan, Rooster Cogburn* (1975); *The Shootist* (1976)

MAUREEN O'HARA: *My Irish Molly, Kicking the Moon Around* (1938); *Jamaica Inn, The Hunchback of Notre Dame* (1939); *A Bill of Divorcement, Dance Girl Dance* (1940); *They Met in Argentina, How Green Was My Valley* (1941); *To the Shores of Tripoli, Ten Gentlemen from Westpoint, The Black Swan* (1942); *The Immortal Sergeant, This Land is Mine, The Fallen Sparrow* (1943); *Buffalo Bill* (1944); *The Spanish Main* (1945); *Sentimental Journey, Do You Love Me* (1946); *Sinbad the Sailor, The Homestretch, Miracle of 34th Street, The Foxes of Harrow* (1947); *Sitting Pretty* (1948); *Britannia Mews, A Woman's Secret, Father was a Fullback, Baghdad* (1949); *Comanche Territory, Tripoli, Rio Grande* (1950); *Flame of Araby* (1951); *At Sword's Point, Kangaroo, The Quiet Man, Against All Flags, Redhead from Wyoming* (1952); *War Arrow* (1953); *Fire Over Africa* (1954); *The Long Gray Line, The Magnificent Matador, Lady Godiva* (1955); *Lisbon, Everything But the Truth* (1956); *The Wings of Eagles* (1957); *Our Man in Havana* (1959); *The Parent Trap, The Deadly Companions* (1961); *Mr Hobbs Takes a Vacation* (1962); *Spencer's Mountain, McLintock* (1963); *The Battle of the Villa Fiorita* (1965); *The Rare Breed* (1966); *How Do I Love Thee* (1970); *Big Jake,* (1971); *The Red Pony* (1972)

BARRY FITZGERALD: *Juno and the Paycock* (1930); *When Knights Were Bold, The Plough and the Stars* (1936); *Ebb Tide* (1937); *Bringing Up Baby, Marie Antoinette, Four Men and a Prayer, The Dawn Patrol* (1938); *The Saint Strikes Back, Pacific Liner, Full Confession* (1939); *The Long Voyage Home* (1940); *San Francisco Docks, The Sea Wolf, How Green Was My Valley, Tarzan's Secret Treasure* (1941); *The Amazing Mrs Holliday, Two Tickets to London, Corvette K225* (1943); *Going My Way, I Love a Soldier, None but the Lonely Heart* (1944); *Incendiary Blonde, And Then There Were None, Duffy's Tavern, The Stork Club* (1945); *Two Years Before the Mast, California* (1946); *Easy Come Easy Go, Welcome Stranger, Variety Girl* (1947); *The Sainted Sisters, The Naked City, Miss Tatlock's Millions* (1948); *Top o' the Morning, The Story of Seabiscuit* (1949); *Union Station* (1950); *Silver City* (1951); *The Quiet Man* (1952); *Happy Ever After, Tonight's the Night* (1954); *The Catered Affair* (1956); *Rooney* (1957); *Broth of a Boy* (1959)

Sources

The author thanks Lord Killanin for access and permission to use material from his files which he kindly made available at his Dublin home. Without his help and courtesy this story would have been left half told.

Anderson, Lindsay,   *About John Ford* (1981)

Brown, Terence,   *Ireland: A Social and Cultural History, 1922 to the Present* (1985)

Carpozi, George,   *The John Wayne Story* (1974)

Fleischer, Nat,   *The Heavyweight Championship* rev. ed. (1961)

Ford, Dan,   *The Unquiet Man: The Life of John Ford* (1982)

Johnson, Jack,   *Jack Johnson – In the Ring and Out* (USA 1927, UK 1977)

Lloyd, Ann, &
Robinson, David,   *Movies of the Fifties* (1984)

McBride, Joseph, &
Wilmington, Michael,   *John Ford* (1975)

McLaglen, Victor,   *Express to Hollywood* (1934)

Macpherson, Don,   *Leading Ladies* (1986)

Matheson, Steve,   *Maurice Walsh, The Storyteller* (1985)

Michael, Paul,   *The Academy Awards: A Pictorial History* 2nd rev. ed. (1972)

Morton, H. V.,   *The Magic of Ireland* (1978)

Norman, Barry,   *The Film Guests* (1985)

The Movie Greats (1981)

Talking Pictures: The Story of Hollywood (1987)

Oram, Hugh,   *Where to go in the West of Ireland* (1984)

Parrish, Robert,   *Growing up in Hollywood* (1976)

Robertson, Patrick,   *Guiness Book of Movie Facts and Feats* 3rd ed. (1988)

Sarris, Andrew,   *The John Ford Movie Mystery* (1976)
Shale, Richard,   *Academy Awards* 2nd ed. (1982)
Shaw, Sam,   *John Wayne in the Camera Eye* (1980)
Shepherd, Donald, & others,   *Duke: the Life and Times of John Wayne* (1986)

Shipman, David,   *The Great Movie Stars – The Golden Years* rev. ed. (1979)

Sinclair, Andrew,   *John Ford* (1979)
Sinyard, Neil,   *Directors: The All-time Greats* (1985)
Tomkies, Mike,   *The Big Man: The John Wayne Story* (1971)
Walsh, Maurice,   *Green Rushes* (1935) – *The Quiet Man*, first appeared in the *Saturday Evening Post* in February 1933 as a short story

Wayne, Pilar, &
Throleifson, Alex,   *John Wayne: My Life with the Duke*
Zmijewsky, Steven,   *Complete Films of John Wayne* (1985)
Zolotow, Maurice,   *John Wayne, Shooting Star* (1974)